SMASHING IDOLS
and
EXPOSING LIES

SMASHING IDOLS

and

EXPOSING LIES:

HOW THE AMERICAN PEOPLE ARE BEING DECEIVED ABOUT VIRTUALLY EVERYTHING

GEORGE PRAZAK

Hardcover ISBN: 979-8-9927400-1-1
Paperback ISBN: 979-8-9927400-0-4
eBook ISBN: 979-8-9927400-2-8

DEDICATED TO:

OUR LOVING HEAVENLY FATHER
OUR LORD AND SAVIOR, JESUS CHRIST
OUR TEACHER AND COMFORTER, THE HOLY SPIRIT

SPECIAL THANKS TO:

My mother and father, who taught me the importance of honesty, and who sacrificed everything, so that I could live in a free country rather than a Communist police state.

One extraordinary woman I have been blessed to know. She is kind, generous, her first name starts with the letter H, and she knows who she is.

Zach, who generously shared his time to teach me the basics of word processing.

The John Hus Presbyterian church family in Binghampton, New York, who welcomed an immigrant family with open arms, and made us feel at home.

SPECIAL MENTION OF SOME WHO TAUGHT AND INSPIRED ME:

John MacArthur

Voddie Baucham

Chuck Missler

Ken Ham

Jason Lisle

Kent Hovind

Justin Peters

Ray Comfort

Mike Winger

Frank Turek

Walter Martin

C.S. Lewis

Frederic Bastiat

Immanuel Velikovsky

G. Edward Griffin

Aaron Russo

Henry M. Morris

Duane Gish

Harold Slusher

Don Patton

Harry Browne

Tucker Carlson

PERSONAL NOTE:

My life's journey has been an extraordinary winding road with many difficult challenges. As a young man, I had an encounter with my Creator, which made me see myself and the world in a different light. Even in the darkest moments of my journey, I never felt truly alone, because the best of friends was walking with me. I was faithless more times than I care to remember, but He remained faithful, and often carried me. My greatest desire is to tell the world about my wonderful friend.

NOTABLE QUOTES:

*"It's easier to fool people than to convince them
that they have been fooled."*
Mark Twain

*"Make the lie big, make it simple, keep saying it,
and eventually they will believe it."*
Adolph Hitler

"A lie is a lie, even if everyone believes it."
Unknown

"A nation of sheep will beget a government of wolves."
Edward R. Murrow

"The American people are free to do exactly what they are told."
Ward Churchill

*"Those people who will not be governed by God
will be ruled by tyrants."*
William Penn

*"Once you eliminate the impossible, whatever remains, no matter
how improbable, must be the truth."*
Arthur Conan Doyle

"You shall know the truth, and the truth shall make you free."
Jesus Christ

INTRODUCTION

The history of mankind is a story of lies. They range from simple and seemingly innocent "white" lies, to intricate, grand deceptions, which are woven into the entire fabric of life and which determine much of what we think, say, and do. The world of politics, religion, commerce, science, and all else, has from the beginning been dominated by deceptions of every kind.

Governments throughout time have been deceiving their subjects in order to keep them from rebelling, and at least one side of every war has justified that war by lying. All religions except one are deceptions, because logic dictates there can only be one spiritual truth. Commerce has had its unjust balances from the start, and science is continually being revised as new information becomes available, making today's dogmas tomorrow's falsehoods.

Scheming and deceit are embedded in human nature, and the greater our intellect and influence, the greater our capacity to benefit ourselves and harm others. Most of the misery in the world can be traced to some deception, and at the root of all deception is a lust for money, position, and power.

While some deceptions are easy to spot and expose, others are so complex and multi-faceted, they can enslave societies for generations. In light of the issues we'll be examining, it should be noted that sometimes even master deceivers fail to achieve their objectives, because all the plans and schemes of evil men and the devil himself, are ultimately subordinate to the plans and purposes of God.

20/20 means perfect clarity of vision, so it should not surprise us that the year bearing this number had been chosen to blind and deceive the entire world. The globalist cabal that has been running things for a long time and that is behind the staged events of 2020, is very fond of numbers and symbols. They particularly like to telegraph what they're about to do, that being their trademark signature. They believe this gives them greater power to confuse, mesmerize, and enslave the masses. As strange as it seems, hiding their agenda in plain sight has been a strategy that has served them quite well.

On the surface, the chaos and madness we see in America today seem to make no sense. There's an explanation for everything, but the answers don't always lie on the surface, and they're not always the answers we want to hear. To get a clearer picture of what is happening today, we need to go back to the beginning, because the problem at its core is a spiritual one, and it began a long time ago.

I will attempt to simplify many complex topics, each of which needs volumes to do them justice, and present only an easily understandable overview. For those wishing to do further research, I will suggest some resources to help. All Scriptural references will be taken from the New American Standard Bible.

Our society is drowning in a sea of lies and delusions, and it is these that have made the events of 2020 possible. Many of them have been with us for generations, and we now accept them as facts and cultural norms that must not be questioned. Perhaps the strongest delusion today is that we're a free people. Under the cover of this one, we have slowly been stripped of many of our God-given rights and are well on our way to losing them all.

Our society is also drowning in a sea of idolatry, the sin most hated by God. Idols have been with us since Adam's fall, and when we see that word, we usually think of statues or images being worshiped by primitive people. They are certainly that, but idols come in an endless variety of forms. Many people would be surprised to learn that the Biblical definition of an idol is anything which we are more devoted to than our Creator. Idols can therefore even be good things which we elevate above their rightful place. For the past few decades, there isn't much that we have elevated more than a talking box called television. Is there anything to which we devote more of our free time, and that has a greater influence on our beliefs and worldview than this box? It is the greatest corporate idol of our time, and perhaps of all time. It is also an idol factory, which has been expertly used to orchestrate the events of 2020 and their devastating aftermath.

In regard to those events, our nation is made up of three types of people; the informed, the confused, and the lost. The informed are those who have a fairly good idea about what happened in 2020. The confused are those who suspect that more happened in 2020 than meets the eye. The largest group are the lost, who don't have a clue and who'd rather not know. The first two types will for the most part be encouraged and helped by this book, but many of the third type will not be helped at all. For various reasons, the *many* have serious problems with truth. When presented with a lie or the truth of practically any issue, many almost always choose the lie. The main reason for this is that in a world of lies, the truth always costs something and sometimes costs everything.

The destiny of America hangs in the balance. The current state of affairs in our nation is disastrous and the hour is late. The good news however, is that it's not too late to get right with the Lord and to stand for truth.

Thank you for taking the time to read this book. It deals with some very uncomfortable truths, but experience has taught me that these are always preferable to comfortable lies. A silver lining can be found even in the greatest darkness, and it's my hope that you will be enlightened, encouraged, and blessed.

George Prazak

TABLE OF CONTENTS

PART ONE:

THE NATURE OF REALITY

DOES GOD EXIST?

Compared to the size of the universe, the earth is smaller than a microscopic speck of dust, and on this speck lives a colony of approximately eight billion two-legged ants. In recent years, a few of the better educated ants have concluded that they are really smart, and they've taken it upon themselves to teach all the rest of the ants about the nature of reality. The "smart" ants now know beyond any doubt that God does not exist, and they feel obligated to share this new, wonderful, and liberating knowledge with all the dumb ants, so that they too can become "smart."

What exactly is it that has convinced the "smart" ants that they're smarter than all previous generations of ants? Modern technological marvels like the computer and the cell phone have certainly played a part, but it's more than that. They have stumbled upon two ideas which caused them to view God as an unnecessary nuisance. These are the Big Bang and Darwin's theory of evolution, sometimes called the two pillars of atheism. The dumb ants are started on this diet very early in life, and before long they're "smart" as well.

The Big Bang is a fascinating concept. We might liken it to the best magic trick ever, but without the magician. The way this magic trick works according to the most educated minds is something like this: At first there was nothing, and at some point that nothing exploded, and became everything. How or by what mechanism nothing became everything has unfortunately never been explained by anyone, and I'm quite certain it never will be. If it could be explained, it would cease to be a magic trick, and those who knew the secret would be creating their own universes, instead of trying to make a name for themselves in this one.

This is what passes for science in today's society, and it is being taught from grade school to the university level. It is zealously promoted by the media and legitimized by endless repetition. Those who promote this idea, mock the Genesis account that God spoke and everything that exists came into being. They believe it makes much more sense that no one spoke and everything that exists came into being. Countless books have been written about it and the discussion will surely continue, but for me to say any more about this absurd, illogical, and thoroughly unscientific idea would be to give it much more credibility than it deserves.

The second pillar is more of a broken crutch than a pillar, but whatever we call it and whatever its lofty scientific pretensions, I hope to show that it is just a facade for a dishonest, fanatical, God-hating cult. It's difficult to know where to even begin when facing such a mountain of suppositions, hoaxes, half-truths, and layers upon layers of deception, spanning more than 160 years. Perhaps we can begin with the name itself.

We've all heard about the theory of evolution, but the term "theory" is somewhat misleading. In order for any scientific idea to be a theory, it must be testable and falsifiable, and due to its nature, evolution doesn't meet either of these criteria. It would be more correct to call it a model or a hypothesis. The reason I even bring this up is because after more than 160 years of being called a theory, it is now being casually referred to as fact. Calling an improvable idea a theory for more than 160 years has given it a status it doesn't deserve, and has created a false impression in people's minds. It would have been much more difficult for people to make the transition from terms like model or hypothesis to fact, than from a term like theory. Whether deliberate or not, this institutionalized deception has definitely changed people's perception of reality.

Before looking at this idea, I'd like to share some fascinating and revealing quotes from leading evolutionists. As you read them, ask yourself whether you're hearing the words of scientists searching for truth, or the words of self-deceived and deceiving cultists:

"Evolution itself is accepted by zoologists not because it has been observed to occur or...can be proved by logically coherent arguments to be true, but because the only alternative, special creation, is clearly incredible." D. M. S. Watson, Biologist

"The probability of life originating from accident is comparable to the probability of the unabridged dictionary resulting from an explosion in a printing shop." Dr. Edwin Conklin, Professor of Biology

"Evolution is unproved and unprovable. We believe it only because the only alternative is special creation, and that is unthinkable." Arthur Keith, Anthropologist

"Scientists who go about teaching that evolution is a fact of life are great con-men, and the story they are telling may be the greatest hoax ever. In explaining evolution, we do not have one iota of fact." Dr. T. N. Tahmisian, Physiologist

"I suppose the reason why we leapt at the Origin of Species was that the idea of God interfered with our sexual mores." Sir Julian Huxley, Biologist

"The extreme rarity of transitional forms in the fossil record persists as the trade secret of paleontology. The evolutionary trees that adorn our textbooks have data only at the tips and nodes of their branches; the rest is inference, however reasonable, not the evidence of fossils." Stephen Jay Gould, Professor of Geology and Paleontology

"Even if all the data point to an intelligent designer, such an hypothesis is excluded from science because it is not naturalistic." Scott Todd, Immunologist

"I still think that, to the unprejudiced, the fossil record of plants is in favor of special creation." E. J. Corner, Professor

"Evolution is promoted by its practitioners as more than mere science. Evolution is promulgated as an ideology, a secular religion – a full-fledged alternative to Christianity, with meaning and morality. I am an ardent evolutionist and an ex-Christian, but I must admit that in this one complaint – and Mr. Gish is but one of many to make it, the literalists are absolutely right. Evolution is a religion. This was true of evolution in the beginning, and it is true

of evolution still today." Michael Ruse, Professor of Zoology and Philosophy

"The belief that life on earth arose spontaneously from non-living matter, is simply a matter of faith in strict reductionism and is based entirely on ideology." Hubert P. Yockey, Physicist and Information Theorist

"We take the side of science in spite of the patent absurdity of some of its constructs.....we are forced by our a priori adherence to material causes to create an apparatus of investigation and set of concepts that produce material explanations, no matter how counter-intuitive, no matter how mystifying to the uninitiated. Moreover, that materialism is absolute, for we cannot allow a Divine Foot in the door." Richard Lewontin

"The more one studies paleontology, the more certain one becomes that evolution is based on faith alone; exactly the same sort of faith which is necessary to have when one encounters the great mysteries of religion. The only alternative is the doctrine of special creation, which may be true, but irrational." Louis T. Moore

".....evolution is the backbone of biology and biology is thus in the peculiar position of being a science founded on an unproven theory. Is it then a science or a faith? Belief in the theory of evolution is thus exactly parallel to belief in special creation. Both are concepts which the believers know to be true, but neither, up to the present, has been capable of proof." Dr. L. H. Mathews

"The hypothesis that life has developed from inorganic matter is, at present, still an article of faith." J. W. N. Sullivan

These quotes are just a tiny sampling, but they are representative of how most *informed* evolutionists feel about their "theory." When they gather together at symposiums and conferences, or communicate with each other through scientific journals, they tend to be quite open about their doubts. It's only when they speak to the public or teach your children that they speak with absolute certainty, and ridicule those who don't buy their story. So, let's take a look at their story, to see if they have any grounds for ridiculing anyone.

There are only two explanations for the existence of life on earth. They are evolution and creation. Neither is, or ever can be a scientific theory, for the reason already stated. They are simply different interpretations of the facts of nature, and much like a jury, we get to decide which interpretation of the facts best describes the world we live in. For many centuries, creation was the dominant view, but with the advent of the Enlightenment that view began to be challenged. It was during this time that Charles Darwin came along.

In 1859, Charles Darwin published his book *On the Origin of Species*, which proposed that all life arose from a single cell, purely through natural processes. Underlying that idea however, was another idea. That the single cell came into being from non-living matter, a primordial chemical soup.

The idea that life can arise spontaneously from non-life was not new in Darwin's day. Aristotle popularized the concept more than 2,000 years earlier, and until the 17th century, many people, including scientists, believed that rotting meat spawned maggots, dust spawned fleas, and rotting flour and cheese spawned mice. Italian scientist Francesco Redi finally performed some experiments in the year 1668, and put that ridiculous notion to rest. It wasn't until Louis Pasteur came along however, that the idea of microbes arising from non-living matter was finally disproved. He did so in 1859, the very year Charles Darwin's book was published! It seems that some false ideas just won't die.

Since Darwin's book was published, evolutionists have been trying to keep alive the idea of the spontaneous generation of life. Despite Pasteur's conclusive experiments on the matter, they can't let it go, because the only alternative explanation for the existence of life is one they don't wish to consider.

In 1859, and for a few decades following, a cell was thought to be just a blob of protoplasm, but today there is no excuse for such ignorance. We now know that the simplest cell, the prokaryote bacteria, is more complex than the space shuttle. It is a virtual city, teeming with activity. A city of factories, transport systems, power plants, and molecular machines performing various functions necessary for life. Here are just a few observations about this incredible biological marvel: The coordinating center for the cell is the DNA molecule. It is a library of information about every constituent part of the organism, and has its own four letter language. The four letters are ATGC, which stand for the chemical bases adenine, thymine, guanine, and cytosine. It is also an incredibly complex software program, which is far more advanced than any invented by man. Among various other functions, the program relays instructions for the construction of proteins and molecular machines, as well as for repair and self-replication. One obvious question to ask is: *Can codes or languages evolve from chemicals?*

Charles Darwin proposed the following way his idea could be disproved: "*If it could be demonstrated that any complex organ existed, which could not possibly have been formed by numerous, successive, slight modifications, my theory would absolutely break down.*" Biochemist Michael Behe, in his book *Darwin's Black Box*, makes the case that the molecular machines just mentioned demonstrate exactly that. They possess what is known as *irreducible complexity*, which simply means that no component of the machine can be missing without the whole ceasing to function.

Does any of the astounding biotechnology of just a simple cell look like the product of some chemicals sloshing around in some primordial soup, or is it the signature of an intelligence beyond our comprehension? Creationists see this as a vindication of their model, but it is a conundrum and a headache for evolutionists. It makes perfect sense therefore that they're fighting like the devil (pun intended) to keep it from the public, and out of the schools. It's also one of the reasons they no longer like to debate creationists. Years before the discovery of molecular machines, evolutionist Niles Eldredge admitted in his 1982 book *The Monkey Business*, that the creation-evolution debates are almost always won by creationists. How often does the media share *this* truth with the American people?

Charles Darwin spun some fanciful tales in his famous book, but he was honest enough on a few occasions to admit that his ideas contradicted what he saw with his own eyes. Before I share a couple of these admissions, I should tell you that die-hard evolutionists get extremely upset when these admissions come to light. They accuse creationists of quoting their hero out of context, saying that if you read his whole book, you'll see that he answered his own doubts. Yes, it's true that he tried to come up with explanations for why his "theory" doesn't match up with observable facts, but they make as much sense as the current evolution nonsense. True science is acknowledging observable facts and following them wherever they lead. *Trying to explain them away is pseudo-science, and engaging in pseudo-science for more than 160 years is a massive, deliberate fraud.*

Having said that, here's another fascinating quote from Mr. Darwin: "*Why, if species have descended from other species by insensibly fine gradations, do we not everywhere see innumerable transitional forms? Why is not all nature in confusion instead of the species being as we see them, well defined?*"

Why indeed? What we see in the fossil record and in nature is exactly what the creation model predicts we would see, but it completely contradicts the evolution model. What Mr. Darwin is asking in his first question is much more profound than what can be answered with a few disputed transitional forms. What he's asking is why isn't there an entire chain of these fossils under our feet, so that we can't tell where one species ends and another begins. In his second question, he is asking why the same isn't true in the real world today, so that we can't tell where one plant or animal ends and another begins. If the process of evolution has been going on for millions of years, why isn't it happening all around us today? With these two simple questions, Charles Darwin pointed out what every objective observer can see. *The fossil record as well as nature only confirm the Genesis account of creation!*

Since people have been digging, billions of fossils have been unearthed, so no one can say there is a shortage of fossils. Yet all of them appear fully formed, which brings up the question, *where are their ancestors?* Thousands of successive generations of plants and animals must have preceded the fossils we've found, so why have their ancestors not been found as well?

How do evolutionists deal with the fossil problem? They deal with it in the same way that they deal with all the other problems of their model. Mostly by ignoring it or talking around it, as they desperately hope that recruits for their cult don't apply critical thinking, and that they swallow their story hook, line, and sinker. The best recruits of course are the very young, which reminds me of a mother who was faced with the challenge of evolution in the life of her eight-year old son. He came home from school one day, fully convinced that the Bible couldn't be true because we evolved from apes. She tried to tell him that's not so, and his answer was classic. "*But Mom, they have pictures, I've seen them!*" That's one thing we have to give the evolutionists. They do have some beautiful pictures with accompanying fairy tales, and with these alone they've managed to brainwash generations of children. Some of these children are now teachers and professors, brainwashing the next generation.

If you run into any of these teachers or professors, you may wish to ask them the following question: *Which came first, the flower or the bee?* The correct answer of course is that both of them must have come into existence at the same time, because neither can survive without the other. The flower and the bee have what is known as a symbiotic relationship. In fact, all living organisms on our planet are dependent on other organisms to one degree or another, and none of them could have waited for millions of years for the others to evolve. *The entire ecosystem is an unbroken chain of interdependent relationships!* Based upon this obvious and undisputed fact alone, is it possible to reach any other conclusion than that all life on our planet came into existence at the same time? The interdependence of all living organisms is essentially a death blow to the very notion of evolution, and all discussion beyond this point is largely irrelevant. It's time to challenge those teachers and professors, because no evolutionist has an answer for this impossible dilemma.

So, how did a massive lie like evolution ever get foisted upon the world? There are many answers to that question, and I'll only mention some of them. One answer is that people in general and the intelligentsia in particular have an aversion to an all-powerful, all-knowing God to whom they are morally accountable. According to polls, about 64% of all scientists are either atheists or agnostics. Other polls indicate that about 93% of the members of the National Academy of Sciences are atheists. This means that scientists in general have a bias against creation, and for evolution. How did they get this bias? They got it from their professors, most of whom were atheists and evolutionists as well, and they in turn got it from their professors. It is a generational cycle of brainwashing that goes all the way back to Charles Darwin, who didn't invent atheism, but who gave atheists something to lean on. Secondly, most people defer to scientists and accept their conclusions about virtually everything, because they are better educated than the general public. Thirdly, there are incentives for being an evolutionist. Those who accept evolution are rewarded, while those who don't are marginalized and ridiculed. Finally, and perhaps most importantly, the growth of this cult can be attributed to a massive brainwashing campaign by the government and the media, which has been going on for more than a century.

Let's take a look at just one example of this brainwashing campaign, the greatest American propaganda film. This 1960 film is a staple of the American public education system, and has been highly instrumental in changing our culture. It not only promotes evolution, but it also makes a mockery of the Bible and Christianity. I'm of course speaking of the film called *Inherit the Wind*, a depiction of the most famous trial in American history, best known as the Scopes Monkey Trial.

The first thing you need to know is that almost nothing in the film is true or historically accurate. Not only because the names of the main characters are fictitious, but because the entire production is a nonsensical farce. Deception along with the promotion of evil has been Hollywood's stock in trade from its inception, but in this particular case, Hollywood outdid itself.

The film is an adaptation of a 1955 play, by playwrights Jerome Lawrence and Robert Edwin Lee. It's a story of High School teacher John Scopes, who was tried for teaching evolution in Dayton, Tennessee in 1925. In the opening scene, what appears to be a group of enforcers is walking deliberately and menacingly toward the school, while a slow version of *Old Time Religion* is playing in the background. The enforcers then enter the school, and John Scopes is arrested and hauled off to jail. That would be lie number one. In reality, John Scopes never spent a day in jail. In a later scene, John Scopes is visited in jail by his love interest Rachael Brown, and the impression given is that he's being tried for a capital crime instead of a misdemeanor. Rachael Brown's father, the Reverend Jeremiah Brown, is portrayed as a two-dimensional cartoon character who disowns his daughter for betraying God and for taking up with a heathen. When preaching to a crowd of crazed, religious zealots who are supposed to represent Christians, Jeremiah Brown calls down curses, fire, and damnation upon sinners. If Hollywood put a mustache on him, he'd be indistinguishable from Hitler during one of his psychotic rants. These are further fabrications, because Rachael Brown and Jeremiah Brown never existed, and there were never any crowds of crazed, religious zealots in Dayton, Tennessee in 1925.

So, what really happened all those years ago and what was the Scopes trial about? First of all, we need to understand the historical context. Evolution was an idea going nowhere, so evolutionists were getting desperate and began creating hoaxes. One of the first was Piltdown Man in 1912, followed by Nebraska Man in 1917, and these hoaxes emboldened them. They began introducing evolution into the public schools, where up until this point only creation was taught. In response to this, about twenty states passed laws against the teaching of evolution, and one of those states was Tennessee. The ACLU was looking for a teacher to help challenge those laws, so they put ads in the papers and one of those ads ended up in a Chattanooga newspaper. Here's an excerpt from that ad, which was run on May 4, 1925: *"We are looking for a Tennessee teacher who is willing to accept our services in testing this law in the courts. Our lawyers think a friendly test case can be arranged without costing a teacher his or her job. All we need now is a willing client."*

A prominent Dayton businessman, George Rappleyea, saw the ad and recognized it as an opportunity to stimulate the town's economy. He talked his friend John Scopes into being the teacher the ACLU was looking for. The details were arranged, and John Scopes was mock arrested by his friends. The show had begun.

What made the Scopes trial a worldwide sensation was the participation of two of the biggest names in the country. William Jennings Bryan, a three-time Presidential nominee of the Democrat Party, volunteered to prosecute the case. Bryan was a Christian, an accomplished attorney, and one of the greatest speakers of his time. After hearing of Bryan's participation in the case, Clarence Darrow, one of the top criminal attorneys in the country, volunteered to serve as defense counsel. Darrow was an agnostic who despised Christianity, but he respected Bryan and campaigned for him twice when he ran for president.

Going back to the movie, Bryan arrives in town and is greeted by a marching band and by ecstatic crowds of religious zealots carrying stupid signs. When Darrow arrives, he is greeted by hostile crowds of religious zealots carrying even stupider signs, and in the 1999 remake of the film, it appears that the ignorant yokels don't even know how to spell "monkeys." The truth is that the citizens of Dayton were just as happy to see Darrow as Bryan, because he was going to put their town on the map and because they were genuinely friendly people. Here's an excerpt from the trial transcript in which Clarence Darrow gives his impression of the people of Dayton: "*I don't know as I was ever in a community where my religious ideas differed as widely from the great mass as I have found them since I have been in Tennessee. Yet I came here a perfect stranger and I can say what I have said before that I have not found upon any body's part – any citizen here in this town or outside the slightest discourtesy. I have been treated better, kindlier and more hospitably than I fancied would have been the case in the north.*" Are you beginning to see that this "historical" docudrama is nothing more than a vicious hit piece on Christians, and by extension on the God of the Bible?

But it gets worse. William Jennings Bryan is portrayed as a pompous, ignorant, hypocritical glutton, while Clarence Darrow is portrayed as a noble, intelligent, and generous soul. How much truth is there in these portrayals? In his book *The Great Monkey Trial*, author Sprague deCamp who does not share Bryan's faith and worldview, nevertheless had this to say about him: *"As a speaker, Bryan radiated good humored sincerity. Few who heard him could help liking him"*…. *"In personality he was forceful, energetic, and opinionated but genial, kindly, generous, likable and charming"*… *"He showed a praise-worthy tolerance towards those who disagreed with him"*…. *"Bryan was the greatest American orator of his time and perhaps any time."*

A number of biographies of Bryan confirm this image rather than the image in the film. Bryan also had extensive scientific knowledge and had read *On the Origin of Species* many years prior to the trial. Clarence Darrow on the other hand, made some puzzling statements during the trial, which cast doubt on whether he had any knowledge of evolution at all. He was often condescending toward witnesses and fellow attorneys, he repeatedly interrupted and insulted Judge Raulston, and was cited for contempt of court. Because of his obnoxious behavior, he was not asked to participate in the appeal.

As the story moves along, the fabrications get even more outrageous. All the scenes with Rachael Brown are obviously fiction, because she never existed. The scene with John Scopes in a jail cell at night is fiction as well, but it's worth mentioning. In it, the town's crazed citizens are marching on the jail with signs and torches, while singing *Glory, Glory, Hallelujah*. A window in the jail is broken and the crowd changes the words of the song to call for the hanging of John Scopes. They then change the words again and call for the hanging of Clarence Darrow. It's not difficult to imagine such a lampooning of Christianity in Communist China or Hindu India or Muslim Iran, but this is being done in what is supposedly *Christian* America and your tax dollars are paying for it.

When the two attorneys square off in the courtroom, the pro-evolution and the anti-God propaganda reaches a fever pitch. Bryan is portrayed as a buffoon and Darrow as the wise and scholarly one. Please notice however, that he's not wise or scholarly because he provides a shred of evidence in support of evolution, but because he manages to make a mockery of the Bible, and if the Bible isn't true then evolution must be. This is the perception most people are left with after watching this farce. To reinforce this perception, Bryan is made to look like an incoherent imbecile, even though the trial transcript says otherwise. Some of the dialogue in the courtroom scenes is poetic license taken to a bizarre extreme. In the final courtroom scene, Bryan seems to have a nervous breakdown and starts babbling. Shortly thereafter, he collapses and dies. None of this happened of course, but the Hollywood spell-casters thought it would be a nice, final touch.

One small Hollywood production, one giant leap for evolution that would change American culture permanently. What I hoped to show you by looking at this propaganda film is how cults are created and how cults are maintained. Brainwashing the masses is easier than people think, once you control the media, the schools, and the government. It also helps if you can create an atmosphere of intimidation, if you can stifle dissent and discourage open debate. Now, imagine if what was done in the case of one film, was being done in a thousand ways with every major issue. *It wouldn't take long to brainwash an entire nation about virtually everything!*

The reason evolutionists can look at the same evidence as those who believe in a young earth and come to totally different conclusions, is because of totally different starting assumptions. First of all, they assume the earth is old, and they assume it's old, because they've been told it's old. It's what we've all been told, ad infinitum ad nauseam for more than two hundred years. One can question any other aspect of the evolution scheme and be considered just a little slow. But if one questions the millions and billions of years and believes in a young universe and a young earth, one is considered a lunatic. The idea has become an unshakable dogma of the modern era. It is the most sacred and most defended idol of the evolution cult, because without it, the cult collapses. So, let's see if we can find a sledgehammer.

First, let us perform a little test to demonstrate how powerful mind control and brainwashing can be. Let's pose a question and see if it generates anything that resembles a programmed response. When did dinosaurs become extinct? That's a fairly challenging question, but I think we can agree that of those who have heard anything about this topic, more than 50% of the people would answer without hesitation and with full conviction that it was 65 million years ago. Most of them would also be able to tell you that it happened as a result of an asteroid hitting what is now the Gulf of Mexico. It's quite amazing that so many people would have the same answer about something which supposedly happened 65 million years ago, and which must logically be relegated to the realm of speculation. This shows that even without a shred of evidence, if you repeat something often enough, you can convince most people about almost anything.

There are dozens of ways to measure the age of the universe and the earth, but the favorites of the evolutionists are radiometric dating. Most other dating methods give very young ages, but these particular methods give them ages they like, so naturally these are the only ones they give credence to. The most common radiometric dating methods are Uranium/Lead, Potassium/Argon, Rubidium/Strontium, and Carbon-14. These are used to date rocks and fossils by the rate of decay of the radioactive elements they contain. A number of assumptions are made about initial conditions, environmental factors, and rates of decay, but if those assumptions are wrong, the results are meaningless. All dating methods are imperfect tools to make educated guesses, but radiometric dating methods have some unique problems. Let me share some amazing test results that you'll never read about in the textbooks.

Mt. Etna, Sicily erupted in 122 BC, and when the rock samples were tested by the Potassium/Argon method, they were dated as 170,000 – 330,000 years old. The samples tested after the 1972 eruption of Mt. Etna were dated as 210,000 – 490,000 years old. When Mt. Ngauruhoe erupted in New Zealand in 1954, the samples were dated as 3.3 – 3.7 million years old. The samples from the Hualalai, Hawaii, 1801 eruption were dated as 1.6 million years old. Kilauea in Hawaii erupted in 1959 and the samples were dated as 8.5 million years old. Mt. St. Helens erupted in 1980 and the samples from there were dated as .35 – 2.8 million years old. Different dating methods were used on the same rock strata in the Grand Canyon. Potassium/Argon gave ages of 10 – 117 million years, Rubidium/Strontium gave ages of 1.27 – 1.39 billion years and Uranium/Lead gave an age of 2.6 billion years. These are just a few examples of the anomalies that occur routinely with radiometric dating, but don't be surprised if the cult has an answer for every single one of them. Most of those who belong to the cult are unfazed by anything that contradicts their dogmas.

Carbon-14 is a radiometric dating method which is most often used to date the fossil remains of plants and animals. It's not as popular with evolutionists as it was in the past, because it appears to have some problems as well. Please consider the following examples: In one case, one part of a mammoth was dated as being 29,000 years old, while another part of that mammoth was dated as being 44,000 years old. Shells from living snails were dated as being 27,000 years old, freshly killed seals were dated as being 1,300 years old, living penguins have been dated as being 8,000 years old, etc., etc. Clearly, some of the assumptions of this dating method must be wrong, but it nevertheless points to a recent creation. It is an accepted fact that nothing older than 100,000 years has any Carbon-14 remaining, yet Carbon-14 has been detected in diamonds, which evolutionists believe to be at least a billion years old.

There are many ways of dating the universe and the earth, which show both to be relatively young. You won't read about them in the textbooks of course, because that would defeat the purpose of the brainwashing. We are told that the universe is 13.8 billion years old and that the earth is 4.5 billion years old, but there are some problems with these ages. In the case of the earth, perhaps the most notable one is the recession of the moon. The moon is moving away from the earth at a rate of one and a half inches a year.

This doesn't seem like much, but at that rate, if we go back in time 1.37 billion years, the moon would have been touching the earth! That doesn't work too well for evolutionists, and they must come up with some kind of explanations or secondary assumptions.

It is generally accepted that comets came into existence at the same time as the solar system. Short period comets don't last more than 10,000 years and long period comets don't last more than 100,000 years. So, why are there still any comets around? This is not a problem for creationists, but evolutionists must once again come up with secondary assumptions. The idea they've proposed is that there is a cloud in interstellar space that gives birth to comets. It is known as the Oort cloud, which no one has ever seen and for which there is no proof, but they're absolutely certain it's there. Some evolutionists have even stated that it's up to creationists to prove it's not there! That's quite a proposition. Suppose I told you, it's an absolute fact that there are six-inch pink elephants running around, and if you don't accept it, you must prove to me they don't exist. Would you ever again take anything I said seriously?

Another indication that the earth is young is the amount of salt in ocean water. Each year about 450 million tons of sodium is added to ocean water through erosion, underground seepage, and from the atmosphere. Only about 120 million tons is removed by other natural processes. At the present rate of accumulation, and if the oceans began with no sodium, it would have taken less than 62 million years to reach the present level of saltiness. If however, the oceans are 3 billion years old as is claimed, they should be a salty, slushy mess, deader than the Dead Sea.

There is very little sediment on the ocean floor, which also indicates a young earth. Each year about 20 billion tons of material ends up in the oceans through continental erosion and about one billion is removed through the movement of tectonic plates. At most it's 1,300 feet thick, and that amount would have accumulated in only 12 million years.

The decay of the earth's magnetic field is yet another powerful indication that the earth is not billions of years old. It has been measured for almost two centuries, and we can extrapolate how strong it was in the past. It loses half its strength every 1,400 years, meaning that 20,000 years ago, it would have been too strong for any life to exist. Some years ago, a book called evolution "a theory in crisis," and the decay of the magnetic field is just one reason why.

Soft tissue and blood vessels have recently been discovered in dinosaur bones. That doesn't necessarily mean the earth is young, but it does mean that dinosaurs didn't become extinct 65 million years ago. It's wonderful to put that silly lie out of commission, but it also raises a question. If that decades-old mantra is a lie, can anything else the cult teaches be believed?

There are dozens of additional evidences of a recent creation and a global flood. I'll mention just a few and let you do your own research. Rapid formation of sedimentary rock beds. Polystrate fossils. Marine fossils atop mountains. Galaxies winding themselves up too fast. Numerous planetary and solar anomalies. The discovery of dinosaur DNA. Helium diffusion from radioactive zircons. All of these fit perfectly with the creation model, but evolutionists must come up with an endless number of secondary assumptions to make them fit *their* model. Based on this alone, which one appears to be the better model?

Those who reject the idea of a young universe and a young earth, feel they have an ace in the hole that can't be beat. It's what is known as the distant starlight problem. We can see light from galaxies that are billions of light years distant from earth, and they therefore think that it must have taken billions of years for that light to reach us. That seems to be the simple and logical conclusion to arrive at, but it may not be the correct conclusion. The best way to arrive at the truth of any issue is to hear both sides of an argument. Most people have only heard one side of this one, and very few are aware of the fact that the Big Bang has a distant starlight problem of its own.

The evolution cult is powerful. It has missionaries in the schools, the media, the government, and even in many churches. For over 160 years, they've been preaching their atheistic gospel and spinning fairy tales for the gullible. That with an unlimited amount of time, the spontaneous generation of life from non-life must have happened. That with an unlimited number of planets in the universe, it surely must have happened on one of them. They're fanatically confident that with an unlimited number of secondary assumptions, all observable facts will one day line up with their religion, and that exploring an unlimited number of rabbit holes will eventually yield all the answers. In all this however, the evolutionists deliberately ignore a mountain of evidence which is all around them and which contradicts their fairy tales. They contemptuously dismiss the answer that has been staring them in the face from the start. The one that doesn't tell them what *must* have happened, but what actually *did* happen.

In the beginning God created the heavens and the earth.

HAS GOD SPOKEN?

To answer this question, all we have to do is simply open our eyes. God has spoken to everyone through His creation, because when we look at the wonders of the universe and the beauty of nature, we can't help but see His infinite power, infinite knowledge, and magnificent artistry. In addition to this, God has written His moral Law upon our hearts. That is a great deal of information we all have about God, but has He spoken in other ways?

All the religions of the world claim a special revelation from God, and many have "holy" books to prove it. But inasmuch as these various revelations contradict each other in numerous ways, how are we to know which of them, or if even one of them is true? Without a close second, the Bible is the number one bestseller of all time. It is the most loved and most hated book of all time, so let's look at the Bible first. It claims to be the exclusive Word of God, so if it contains evidence of a divine origin, we won't have to look further.

When atheists promote their religion, they rarely ever mention or attack any other religious book besides the Bible. They have more of a preoccupation with this book and the God of this book than most Christians. The most passionate of them write books, or they're online day after day, sometimes for years. The bulk of their posts and video content is devoted to the Bible, the God of the Bible, Jesus, and Christianity. They claim that their atheism has liberated them, but if this is what being liberated looks like, I'd hate to see bondage. On the one hand, listening to them is somewhat amusing, but on the other hand, it's also heartbreaking. One wonders how it's possible to find satisfaction in peddling the bleakest of all worldviews. *No God, no objective truth, no ultimate standard of morality, no ultimate purpose, no ultimate justice, and no ultimate hope.* Nevertheless, almost all of them will tell you that they became atheists, because evolution made them see the "light."

They make many unsubstantiated claims about the Bible. They claim that it's full of contradictions, that it's historically inaccurate, and that archeology and science have disproved it. Many books have been written, which address all their claims very effectively, so perhaps the atheists aren't being completely honest. In reality, the Bible is the most credible book in the world, and in the next few pages, I hope to show you just how credible it is. One of my main objectives in writing *this* book is to demonstrate that it's dangerous to believe everything we hear, and doubly dangerous to allow other people to do our thinking for us.

First of all, the Bible isn't just one book, but a collection of 66 books. It was written over the span of approximately 2,000 years, on three continents, in three languages, by about 40 authors from different backgrounds. It includes history, law, prophecy, proverbs, parables, poetry, and personal correspondence. Its authors claim that they had a personal encounter with a Supreme Being. They described His character in great detail and recorded His very words. The compilation of these eyewitness reports is absolutely astounding and defies explanation. *Most of them never met and were separated by hundreds of years, yet they all contributed interlocking pieces of one unified story!*

The Bible is the only book that seriously challenges the atheistic worldview, so atheists naturally attack it. Alleging Bible contradictions is one of their favorite lines of attack, but upon closer examination, this line of attack fails miserably. Some contradictions they invent are nothing more than words and verses being taken out of context, but by that method it's possible to make anything appear like a contradiction. Other alleged contradictions are related to translation issues, but checking the original languages clears them up quite easily. Still others, are simply the adding or omitting of details by different authors, as sometimes happens in the Gospels. And finally, some alleged contradictions are just plain silly. An example of a silly one would be juxtaposing the words "*with God all things are possible,*" and the words "*it is impossible for God to lie.*" Exactly like Clarence Darrow in the Scopes trial, atheists feel that the best way to vindicate their worldview is to discredit the opposition, and they're busy as bees trying to do just that. For those who want the answer to every alleged Bible contradiction, I suggest the book *Keeping Faith In An Age Of Reason*, by Jason Lisle.

How many times have you heard the line, "science has disproved the Bible"? Those who make such statements are really talking about evolution, which for them is an undisputed scientific fact. Other than evolution, which is very much in dispute, the Bible is amazingly accurate when it comes to science. It's not a science textbook, but it does reveal knowledge of the natural world, which people living thousands of years ago could not possibly have had.

Here are a few scientific insights that can be found in the Bible:

An expanding universe. ----- For thousands of years, it was the accepted view among all but Bible believers that the universe is static. That view changed in 1929, when Edwin Hubble proved conclusively that the universe is expanding. This is what the Bible says: "*Who stretches out the heavens like a curtain And spreads them out like a tent to dwell in.*" Isaiah 40:22, Additional verses: Isaiah 42:5, 44:24, 45:12, Jeremiah 10:12, 51:15, Job 9:8, 37:18, Zechariah 12:1

The earth free floats in space. ----- Many cultures and some religions held very peculiar notions about the earth. Some believed that the earth sits on the backs of elephants or turtles. In 1475, Copernicus discovered that the earth free floats in space. This is what the Bible says: "*He stretches out the north over empty space, And hangs the earth on nothing.*" Job 26:7

The earth is round. ----- Greek philosophers first mentioned a spherical earth around 500 BC. In the time of Isaiah the prophet, about 200 years earlier, this is what the Bible said: "*It is He who sits above the circle of the earth.*" Isaiah 40:22, Additional verses: Job 26:10 (around 2,000 BC), Proverbs 8:27

Springs in the sea. ----- Water springs were discovered on the ocean floor in the 1970's. This is what the Bible says: "*Have you entered into the springs of the sea? Or have you walked in the recesses of the deep?*" Job 38:16

Ocean currents. ----- Oceanography became a science in the 1800's and ocean currents were charted. This is what the Bible says: "*Whatever passes through the paths of the seas.*" Psalm 8:8

Wind currents. ----- Meteorology became a science in the 1800's and wind currents were charted. This is what the Bible says: "*Blowing toward the south, Then turning toward the north, The wind continues swirling along; And on its circular courses the wind returns.*" Ecclesiastes 1:6

Air has weight. ----- In the 1600's, it was discovered that air has weight. This is what the Bible says: "*When He imparted weight to the wind.*" Job 28:25

The water cycle. ----- The water cycle was not understood until the 1600's, but this is what the Bible says: "*For He draws up the drops of water, They distill rain from the mist, Which the clouds pour down, They drip upon man abundantly.*" Job 36:27-28, Additional verses: Amos 9:6, Ecclesiastes 1:7

The number of stars is innumerable. ----- About 2,000 stars are visible with the naked eye. With telescopes, we now know that there are hundreds of billions of galaxies, with an average of 100 billion stars in each. This is what the Bible says: "*As the host of heaven cannot be counted.*" Jeremiah 33:22

Every star is completely different. ----- Until telescopes were invented, the accepted view was that all stars were basically the same. Now we know that no two stars are the same. This is what the Bible says: "*Star differs from star in glory.*" 1 Corinthians 15:41

Blood is the source of life. ----- This fact was not discovered until modern medicine came along, but this is what the Bible says: "*For the life of the flesh is in the blood.*" Leviticus 17:11

The optimal time for circumcision. ----- The blood-clotting agents vitamin K and prothrombin are at their peak on the eighth day. This is what the Bible says: "*And on the eighth day the flesh of his foreskin shall be circumcised.*" Leviticus 12:3

The Bible also has lists of hygiene rules, dietary laws, and quarantine protocols, which have all been validated by modern medical discoveries. Not one word of it has ever been disproved. Can any one person or any group of people in the ancient world have had such extensive scientific knowledge, or is this the signature of an all-knowing God?

Inventing Bible contradictions in order to mislead people is one thing, but denying a mountain of evidence and telling outright lies is a completely different level of deception. It occurs most often when it comes to Biblical history and archaeology. You cannot imagine the desperation of those who feel compelled to destroy the Bible's credibility, and the lengths they'll go to in order to achieve that end. There are some who actually deny that the Hebrews ever sojourned in ancient Egypt, so that they wouldn't have to explain the Exodus. There are still others, who deny that King David and King Solomon ever existed. For a long time, the same type of people mocked the Bible, because it mentions Hittites. In 1906 however, the joke was turned on them. That year, archaeologists discovered that the Hittites not only existed, but that they had a mighty empire encompassing most of Turkey and parts of the Middle East.

Today, those who deny the reality of the Exodus, or of David and Solomon, are either hopelessly out of touch or shameless liars. In 1978, archaeologist and researcher Ron Wyatt discovered the remains of four, six, and eight spoke chariot wheels on the seafloor of the Gulf of Aqaba. Don't be surprised however, to learn that this spectacular find has been labeled a hoax by some professional liars. Yes, lying has actually become a business in our society, and we'll address this more fully in later chapters. One of the most amusing lies regarding this discovery is that Ron Wyatt put those chariot wheels down there himself!

There are hundreds of archaeological digs in Israel, and they have done nothing but confirm the accuracy of Scripture down to the smallest detail. Despite the mountain of evidence which has been accumulated, the skeptics and mockers are not impressed in the least. If they're not outright denying some discovery, their main argument seems to be that *everything* hasn't yet been found, so that what *has* been found has no validity. I'll mention a few of the thousands of finds: Joshua's altar on Mt. Ebal, stones from the Jordan at Gilgal, the "house of David" inscription, the Balaam inscription, the fortified gates of Solomon, Jeroboam's altar at Dan, and the fallen walls of Jericho. In addition, the City of David was discovered, and it contains the following: Administration buildings, the tombs of David and Solomon, the coronation site of Solomon, Joab's water shaft, Gihon spring, the pool of Melchizedek, the pool of Siloam, the tower of Siloam, Hezekiah's walls, Nehemiah's rebuilt walls, stairs from the temple to the pool, and the palace of David which is almost two hundred yards long and six stories high! Finally, the ruins of Sodom and Gomorrah have been discovered, as has the *real* Mt. Sinai, which is located in Saudi Arabia. Will any of this convince those who have made up their minds not to be convinced? Probably not, because their problem doesn't seem to be an intellectual one, but a moral one. It isn't so much that they've found any evidence that the Bible isn't true, but rather that they don't *want* it to be true.

If a book accurately predicted the future 100% of the time, that would be considered powerful evidence of being divinely inspired. About a quarter of the Bible is prophecy, and it has never been wrong. It predicted the rise and fall of nations and empires, as well as coming judgments, military invasions, and the outcomes of wars. It not only gives us the history of the world, but it predicted the future of the world. In particular, the future of the nation of Israel. For example, it predicted the destruction of Jerusalem and its Temple in 70 AD, and the subsequent dispersion of the Jewish people around the world. It also predicted that they would be gathered back together at the end of the age, and that the nation of Israel would be restored. This happened in 1948, more than 2,500 years after those prophecies were made. Since becoming a nation, many more prophecies have been fulfilled.

The dominant theme of the first portion of the Bible is that God Himself would come to earth in the person of the Messiah. The Old Testament prophesies His coming, and the New Testament heralds His arrival. Jesus of Nazareth fulfilled over 100 prophecies that pertain to the coming Messiah. Mathematics professor Peter Stoner, along with 600 of his students, calculated the probability of any person fulfilling just 48 of those prophecies. They assigned very conservative numerical values to each of the prophecies, and this is the calculation they came up with: The probability of those 48 prophecies being fulfilled by any single person is one chance in 10^{157}! That is 10, followed by 157 zeros. To give you an idea of how large a number that is, the estimated number of atoms in the universe is 10^{80}. Another way of putting it is that there's only one chance in 10^{157} that Jesus is *not* the promised Messiah!

This should be enough to convince anyone, but there is much, much more. There are numerous authenticating patterns and messages in the Bible that are buried beneath the actual text. I will share only one amazing message. Many Biblical names have very specific meanings, and there is something extraordinary that has been discovered in a genealogy in the book of Genesis. It starts with Adam which means man, followed by Seth which means appointed, followed by Enosh which means mortal, followed by Kenan which means sorrow, followed by Mahalalel which means the blessed God, followed by Jared which means shall come down, followed by Enoch which means teaching, followed by Methuselah which means his death shall bring, followed by Lamech which means despairing, followed by Noah which means comfort. Putting all that together in one sentence, we get the following message: MAN (is) APPOINTED MORTAL SORROW (but) THE BLESSED GOD SHALL COME DOWN TEACHING (that) HIS DEATH SHALL BRING (the) DESPAIRING COMFORT. God had hidden the summary of the Christian Gospel in a genealogy in the first book of the Bible! This is just a tiny glimpse into the infinite mind of God!

To summarize, Jesus Christ is the most significant person who ever lived, and the obvious evidence of that is that He split history in half and that our calendar dates back to His birth. The Bible is the most significant book in the world, because directly and indirectly, it is all about Him. After reading the last few pages, can anyone honestly say that there is any book in the world that is in any way comparable to the Bible?

With all the evidence that the Bible is the inspired Word of God, why do so many people reject it? One reason is that there is a massive disinformation campaign about this book that appeals to people. The Bible has a unique quality, which no other book in the world has. While we are reading it, it is at the same time reading us and examining the innermost parts of our being. That is much more examination than most sinners care for, and as our cultural morality declines, so does the love for this book.

Atheists, Bible mockers, and God-haters can post countless videos, write countless books, and make countless jokes, but none of that will ultimately accomplish a thing. God has made Himself abundantly known to all through His creation and through His Law written on our hearts. Many have the additional revelation of His written Word. Even if every person on earth were to rise up in rebellion against Him, nothing would change, because *He* cannot change. God has indeed spoken in ways that no one can miss, but some pretend not to hear Him, and some shake their fists at Him.

THE GREAT COSMIC CONFLICT

If God is good, why is there so much evil in the world? That's a question that has brought much confusion to many. Some people speculate that God is good, but not all-powerful. Others speculate that God is all-powerful, but not good. It's an endless cycle of speculation that answers nothing and only fuels the confusion. The only one who knows the answer to this question is God Himself, and He has given us that answer in His Word. If people simply opened the Bible and started reading it, the world would shortly begin to make much more sense to them.

God is the source of all life, truth, and goodness. He is eternally complete and has need of nothing. That of course raises the question of why He chose to create. The only answer the Bible provides is that it pleased Him to do so, and anything beyond this is mere speculation. In any case, the Lord did create, and while it is clear from Scripture that He wishes to have a loving relationship with all His creatures, it would be a mistake to think that He *needs* love from any of them.

If the Lord needed to be loved, He could easily have made creatures who could do nothing else but love Him. But would that really be love? Doesn't love require a choice? So, the Lord created

His highest orders of creatures as free moral agents who could choose, which carried with it the possibility that some of them would reject Him. To those who would make the choice to love the Lord, He promised a blissful eternity in His presence. To those who would make the choice not to love the Lord, He promised a much less pleasant eternity apart from Him.

One of the creatures who did not choose to love the Lord was a high ranking angel by the name of Lucifer. He chose instead to love himself. He resented the Lord for having authority over him and became filled with pride. This was ultimately his downfall, which is why pride is considered to be the deadliest of all sins. It opens the door to all other sins, because it blinds us to what we are and deceives us into believing we're something that we are not.

In the case of Lucifer, his pride led to the sin of rebellion that a third of all the angels joined. It was then that God changed his name from Lucifer which means light bearer, to Satan which means adversary. He made his first appearance in the book of Genesis in the form of a serpent. The Lord had just pronounced His creation "*very good*," and it was Satan's intention to corrupt that creation by spreading his rebellion to earth. This is when he approached our first mother Eve.

For those unfamiliar with the story, the Lord arranged a test for Adam and Eve to see if they would trust and obey Him. He created a beautiful Garden for them, where He planted every kind of tree for them to enjoy. He placed just one restriction on them. "*From any tree of the garden you may eat freely; but from the tree of the knowledge of good and evil you shall not eat, for in the day that you eat from it you shall surely die.*" Genesis 2:16-17. Satan showed up some time later, but he was crafty enough not to approach Adam and Eve when they were together. Together they might have seen through his trickery, so when Eve was alone, he made his move.

Satan's strategy was brilliant, and it worked so well, he's been using it ever since on everyone. The first thing he did was to ask Eve a seemingly innocent question, but it was anything but innocent. *"Indeed, has God said, 'You shall not eat from any tree of the garden'?"* Genesis 3:1. He knew very well that's not what God said, but it planted the seed of rebellion in Eve's mind. It got her to question God's character and to consider the possibility that perhaps He was being too restrictive. The fact that her mind was going in this direction is evident from her response. *"From the fruit of the trees of the garden we may eat; but from the fruit of the tree which is in the middle of the garden, God has said, 'You shall not eat from it or touch it, lest you die.'"* Genesis 3:2-3. Very casually, she attributed to God an additional command He never gave, and at that point the deceiver knew he had her. Before she could correct her error, he said *"You surely shall not die! For God knows that in the day you eat from it your eyes will be opened, and you will be like God, knowing good and evil."* Genesis 3:4-5. He not only lied to her, but essentially called God a liar. He fanned the tiny spark of rebellion he planted, by implying that God was withholding something good and desirable. Satan's temptation centered on self-will and pride, the very things that caused *his* downfall. It wouldn't be long before Eve came to realize that knowing evil was not desirable at all.

"When the woman saw that the tree was good for food, and that it was a delight to the eyes, and that the tree was desirable to make one wise, she took from its fruit and ate; and she gave also to her husband with her, and he ate. Then the eyes of both of them were opened, and they knew that they were naked; and they sewed fig leaves together and

made themselves loin coverings." Genesis 3:6-7. The rebellion was underway, and the first consequences of that rebellion were evident immediately. Those consequences were loss of innocence and shame, but that was just the beginning. Mankind was about to embark upon a 6,000-year voyage into darkness and deception, captained by *"the father of lies."* Our first parents joined Satan in his rebellion against the Lord, and they passed on that rebellion to all their descendants. This is why the Bible also calls Satan *"the god of this world."* When we see the world's evil, it shouldn't be too difficult to figure out who to blame. First and foremost, Satan for deceiving us in some way, and secondly ourselves for believing his lies.

Adam and Eve did not die physically the day they ate the forbidden fruit, but they did die spiritually. Their relationship with the Lord was severed. *"Then the Lord God called to the man, and said to him, 'Where are you?' And he said, 'I heard the sound of Thee in the garden, and I was afraid because I was naked; so I hid myself.' And He said, 'Who told you that you were naked? Have you eaten from the tree of which I commanded you not to eat?'"* Genesis 3:9-11. From that point on, mankind has been spiritually separated from God. We were all born spiritually dead, because we've inherited the sin nature of our first parents. The dilemma has been how to find our way back to God.

The bad news is that fallen mankind cannot ever find its way back to God. The good news is that God found a way to us. After finding Adam and Eve hiding, the Lord pronounced judgments on them and on Satan. But hidden in those judgments was the promise of a coming Savior. In later portions of God's Word, we learn that this Savior would pay the penalty for all the sins of all those who would repent and trust in Him. To illustrate that Adam and Eve could not adequately cover their sins, and that a blood sacrifice was needed to cover them, the Lord made garments of *skin* for them. After that, they were cast out of the Garden of Eden, and it has been a downward slide for mankind ever since.

It wasn't long before the first murder was committed, and the issue of religion played a key role. The Lord prescribed the only acceptable form of worship and Cain showed his disdain for it. When his brother's offering to the Lord was accepted and his was not, Cain became angry and killed his brother Abel. What was the difference between the two offerings? Abel's was a sacrifice of an animal from his flock, which symbolized God's perfect blood sacrifice. Cain's was the fruit of the ground, which symbolized some other way to gain God's acceptance. At the core, there are only two religions in the world. One says we can earn salvation by something we do, and the other says it only comes through faith in the sacrifice of the Messiah.

God's plan of salvation and His assessment of us didn't sit well with people from the beginning. Most believe that they are basically good and that their good works will gain them entrance into heaven. The Word of God utterly contradicts this notion, and this is what it has to say about the goodness of all of us: *"as it is written, there is none righteous, not even one, there is none who understands, there is none who seeks for God; all have turned aside, together they have become useless; there is none who does good, there is not even one."* Romans 3:10-12. This passage is a perfect illustration of why people have a hostility toward the Bible. It describes us in a way that we don't see ourselves, but our faulty assessment of ourselves comes from a fundamental misunderstanding of two things. Our sinfulness and God's holiness. Being sinners, can we see our own sins as God sees them, and can we even begin to comprehend His holiness? Does a pig know it's dirty, and does it have a clue about what it means to be clean?

Even though the Lord had sent prophets like Enoch and Noah to the people, they turned their backs on God and became more and more wicked. *"Then the Lord saw that the wickedness of man was great on the earth, and that every intent of the thoughts of his heart was only evil continually."* Genesis 6:5. *"Now the earth was corrupt in the sight of God, and the earth was filled with violence."* Genesis 6:11. For 120 years, Noah was building the Ark, calling people to repentance and warning them about God's coming judgment. When the flood finally came, it was only Noah and his family that boarded it. That's a level of commitment to evil that can only be labeled madness. The world of that day was in total rebellion against a loving God.

There exist two kingdoms, and these have been at war since the beginning. We are fast approaching the final battle of this war, and there's little time left to choose sides. It needs to be understood that we are all born into Satan's kingdom, but the Lord has offered everyone the awesome privilege of switching sides and becoming His children. The catch is that in God's kingdom, there is only one will. Anyone who wishes to be part of it, must give up his own. In Satan's kingdom, there are as many wills as there are beings in it, and this explains why there's so much chaos and evil in the world. Alistair Crowley, the most famous Satanist of the 20th century, wrote that the only commandment in Satan's kingdom is *"do what thou wilt."* Satan offers his followers self-will and pride, exactly as he did with Adam and Eve. Unfortunately, most people find these temptations irresistible.

Shortly after the flood, the rebellion against the Lord started up again at Babel. The Lord told the descendants of Noah to disperse into all the world and to repopulate it. In typical fashion, the people had their own ideas. *"And they said, 'Come, let us build for ourselves a city, and a tower whose top will reach into heaven, and let us make for ourselves a name; lest we be scattered abroad over the face of the whole earth."* Genesis 11:4. This was the first recorded attempt to form a world government and a false world religion. The Lord thwarted this rebellion at Babel by confusing the people's language. He thwarted it many other times in history, but He will allow it for a very brief time at the end of the age. When He does, the consequences for mankind will be catastrophic.

Starting with Cain and seen again at Babel, false religion has been Satan's alternative to the worship of the one true God. There is a spiritual hunger in all of us, but if we reject the Lord, all that is left is some Satanic counterfeit. The deceiver has set up a spiritual marketplace, offering an endless variety of products. They are all essentially the same poison, only with different labels and different doses. He has repackaged ancient paganism into New Age paganism, to accommodate modern sensibilities. Some of the most popular products in his marketplace are Gnosticism, mysticism, the occult, witchcraft, astrology, reincarnation, and higher consciousness. To more primitive people, he offers sun, moon and star worship, nature worship, animal worship, and ancestor worship. To more sophisticated audiences, he offers contact with ascended masters, contact with extraterrestrials, and various cults which peddle what may be the deadliest poison of all, counterfeit Christianity. Satan provides authenticating experiences and miraculous manifestations for all of these, and people tend to believe that makes them right, or even that they come from God. What *all* of the deceiver's products have in common is *no accountability to an all-knowing, all-powerful, personal, holy God!* It's very sad, but Satan's marketplace is quite popular and is doing brisk business.

While chaos, hate, and division are the dominant features of Satan's kingdom, his children always join together in the end against the children of God. Underlying all the conflicts in the world is the fundamental struggle between good and evil, light and darkness, truth and deception. It is a war between the children of God and the children of the devil, but at an even deeper level, it is a war between the children of the devil and God Himself. Christians and Jews represent the God of the Bible, who is the only true God, which is why these two groups of people have been the most hated and persecuted people in history.

From the beginning, the Lord has been calling His fallen, misguided, and rebellious creatures back to Himself. He began His redemptive plan with a man named Abraham, whom He promised to make a great nation. It was through that nation that God's written Word and the Messiah were ordained to come. Despite its wickedness and continual rebellion against the Lord, Israel nevertheless became a light to a dark world steeped in paganism and idolatry. The faithlessness of the children of Israel served as a powerful witness of the mercy and faithfulness of the one true God. The Bible is the story of that witness.

God's written revelation to the world came through the nation of Israel, which is why it's the most hated nation in the world. Satan has done all in his power to wipe the Jewish people off the face of the earth. He could never succeed, because the Lord promised to preserve His covenant people. It was prophesied long ago that the final world conflict would involve Israel and the city of Jerusalem. That day is near, and the great cosmic conflict is coming to its inevitable climax.

The battle lines are being drawn between those who love the Lord and those who hate Him. These lines are becoming clearer with each passing day, as the world races toward Armageddon. We who love the Lord should be encouraged, because we've read the end of the book, and we know who wins. The rest should seriously reexamine *what* they believe and *who* they believe, *before it's too late.*

PART TWO:

DECEPTION

COGNITIVE DISSONANCE

It's been said that a little bit of information can be a dangerous thing, because deception thrives when information is limited. In recent years, the powers that be in our nation have greatly limited our access to information. Whenever or wherever this has been done, it was always done in order to deceive as many people as possible. The most easily deceived of course, are those who don't believe they could ever be deceived. Today, our nation is full of such people, and consequently our society is drowning in lies.

When people are confronted with truth and have their false beliefs thoroughly exposed, it creates an inner conflict which is known as cognitive dissonance. According to the Merriam-Webster Dictionary, the definition of cognitive dissonance is: *"Psychological conflict resulting from incongruous beliefs and attitudes held simultaneously."* The Encyclopedia Britannica has this to say: *"Cognitive dissonance, the mental conflict that occurs when beliefs or assumptions are contradicted by new information. The unease or tension that the conflict arouses in people is relieved by one of several defensive maneuvers: they reject, explain away, or avoid the new information; persuade themselves that no conflict really exists; reconcile the differences; or resort to any other defensive means of preserving stability or order in their conceptions of the world and of themselves.*" The journey from darkness to light is quite often a very uncomfortable experience, but in my opinion, the final destination is worth any and all discomfort.

The comfort zone for most people is to do as little thinking as possible, and to help us reach that comfort zone, we're all greatly aided by the schools, the mainstream media, and the government. All three are committed to protecting us from ever having to experience cognitive dissonance. The only thing the people running these institutions require of us is that we never question them. It would please them greatly if we all avoided libraries, or any other sources of alternative information. By following this regimen carefully, we can be spared the embarrassment of discovering we were ever wrong about anything.

The longer this goes on, the greater the cognitive dissonance if the egg of willful ignorance is broken. It's not too difficult to accept that one was wrong for a few weeks or months, but it's much more difficult to accept that one was wrong for years, or even an entire lifetime. This is why it's almost impossible to fix a society that has been broken for generations. It's also the main reason that the percentage of people converting to Christianity gets smaller and smaller in each decade of life. Most people who get right with the Lord, do so when they're young. We do hear of deathbed conversions, but those occurrences are extremely rare. The point is that it goes against our prideful nature to ever admit to being wrong. Nevertheless, I hope that the remaining chapters will break a few eggs.

There's a fairy tale that many of us are familiar with, which speaks to what happened to our nation in 2020. In fact, I think it was written specifically for us. I'm speaking of *The Emperor's New Clothes*, by Hans Christian Andersen. Here's a quick summary of the story for those who haven't heard it:

There once lived an Emperor who was fond of clothes. In fact, he was obsessed with clothes, and his whole life revolved around being well dressed and admired. In the course of time, two con artists showed up in town and heard about the Emperor's obsession. They immediately passed themselves off as master weavers and tailors. They let it slip that they can weave the most extraordinary fabrics with certain peculiar properties. One of those properties was that they were invisible to people not fit for their office or to fools. The Emperor heard about this, and knew he just had to have a new suit made of this wonderful material. Every Emperor needs to be able to identify fools, so he called for the two scoundrels and commissioned them to make him a new set of clothes. They immediately commenced working the looms, sewing and stitching, but other than their hand gestures, there was nothing to be seen. After some time, the Emperor sent his top minister to check on the progress of the tailors. He could see nothing, but they described the suit in great detail and in glowing terms. They then asked his opinion of their handiwork, and he wishing not to appear a fool, told them the suit was magnificent. He then reported the same to the Emperor. Some time later, the Emperor sent another of his ministers to check on the suit. The same thing happened as happened with the first minister, he couldn't see a thing. But he knew the previous minister had seen the suit, so the only explanation for *him* not seeing it was that he was a fool, and not fit for his office. That would never do, so he told the tailors and the Emperor that the suit was absolutely

49

majestic, the best he'd ever seen. Finally, the Emperor himself went to see the suit and he couldn't see a thing either, but he knew that both his ministers saw the suit and were extremely impressed. So, rather than admit that he couldn't see a thing and be considered a fool who's unfit for his office, he told the con artists what they wanted to hear. It then came time for the Emperor to dress in his new suit and make his customary procession through town, to be admired by all his subjects. Everyone in the empire knew that the entire royal court had highly praised the suit, and they also knew about the suit's mysterious properties. Not wishing to be thought fools or unfit for office, everyone in the crowd went wild with praise for the Emperor's new clothes. And then, the shocking but truthful words were finally uttered:

"'But he hasn't got anything on' a little child said. 'Did you ever hear such innocent prattle?' said its father. And one person whispered to another what the child had said. 'He hasn't anything on. A child says he hasn't anything on.' 'But he hasn't got anything on!' the whole crowd cried out at last. The Emperor shivered, for he suspected they were right. But he thought, 'this procession has got to go on.' So, he walked more proudly than ever, as his noblemen held high the train that wasn't there at all."

This is a story about many things, but primarily it's about pride, gullibility, self-deception, and mindless conformity. It's a story about people sometimes believing and doing the most absurd things, simply because everyone else is believing and doing them. Everyone in the empire was so desperate not to be thought a fool, that they inadvertently allowed a couple of con artists to make fools of all of them! In this context, this story is a perfect illustration of what happened to us in 2020.

If the Corona virus outbreak was not a real pandemic, then a great multitude of people have allowed a very tiny group of people to make fools of them. If the unthinkable is actually true, then this would constitute the greatest deception in recorded history! When it fully comes to light, as it probably will, the consequences are bound to be catastrophic. If it doesn't come to light, the consequences will be even more catastrophic. It's a classic no-win situation. In order to avoid cognitive dissonance and hold on to their pride, many will welcome even more blatant deception, rather than acknowledging the brutal truth!

CONSPIRACY THEORY

CONSPIRACY THEORY! I purposely wrote those words in bold, capital letters to make them three times as scary. As we all know, they seem to evoke a visceral response in us that makes us uncomfortable to even look at them. We don't have a problem with either one of these words separately, but when they're together, they seem to gain some magical power over us. Why is that?

The answer is simple. We have all been part of a mind control experiment and have been conditioned to react that way. We've been indoctrinated by endless repetition to automatically associate these words with crazy ideas and crazy people. Therefore, whenever the government or the media labels anything a conspiracy theory, most people immediately put up a wall and shut down all critical thinking. This is a very ingenious way for our leaders to control us and do virtually anything they want without oversight. By falling for such obvious mental manipulation, the American public has unwittingly become the defender of the greatest evils.

I recall an incident in which I attempted to share some information with a neighbor, who must have been particularly well indoctrinated. Before even hearing a single fact about the issue, her immediate and very angry response was, "where did you get your information, *the internet?*" I knew at once what prompted my neighbor's irrational response, and was tempted to ask, "where did you get *your* information, *the idiot box?*" As frightening as these two words seem to be to some people, it's much more frightening to see how simple, innocent words have been so cunningly manipulated to give them such incredible propaganda power.

The words *"conspiracy theory"* are a nonsensical term that has been employed in the most nonsensical ways. Here's one of a multitude: *"Should Christians believe conspiracy theories?"* That question is not only vague, but it's also utterly ridiculous. One of the reasons it's ridiculous is that inasmuch as the term "conspiracy theories" has become a synonym for "crazy ideas," what's the point of even asking such a question? This is what's known as a leading question, which is designed to elicit only one type of response. Secondly, there's no legitimate reason to substitute a pejorative term for something that is nothing more than an alternative narrative. So, which narratives is the questioner referring to? Are they all in one big bag and we must either accept or reject the entire bag? If it's a narrative that has scant evidence to support it, such as the one about blood-sucking space aliens hiding in people's basements, then I'd say Christians would be wise to discard it. If however, it's a narrative with an overwhelming amount of factual evidence supporting it, then Christians have no choice but to believe it. Rather than focusing on some ridiculous label that certain information has been deliberately tagged with, the issue for Christians should always be whether something is true or not. *Our God is a God of truth, and we as His ambassadors have no business believing and spreading lies!*

Let's look at just one issue that has been tagged with the conspiracy theory label by the professional liars. Fluoride in the tap water. Anyone who talks about it is immediately labeled a crazy conspiracy theorist, so let's see if there's anything crazy about it. I will simply list a few facts regarding the issue. FACT: Fluoride is added to two thirds of America's water supply. FACT: Fluoride is a sedative. FACT: Over 95% of all countries have banned water fluoridation. FACT: Hitler and Stalin fluoridated the water in concentration camps to make prisoners more docile and easier to control. FACT: Fluoridation became the official policy of the U.S. Public Health Service in 1951. Along with the American Dental Association, it launched a propaganda campaign promoting fluoridation. FACT: There is no discernible difference in tooth decay between countries that fluoridate their water and those that don't. FACT: Fluoride is a dangerous neurotoxin that is destructive to brain tissue, the spinal cord, and the nervous system. Among several other adverse health effects, it is also known to lower IQ in children. FACT: There is a health warning on the back of every tube of toothpaste containing fluoride. *"If more than used for brushing is accidentally swallowed, get medical help or contact a Poison Control Center right away."*

Please notice that I haven't theorized about anything, and I haven't accused anyone of conspiring. Nevertheless, the professional liars call these, and many other facts related to fluoride, a conspiracy theory. They do this very thing about every other issue that they don't want anyone to investigate, and most Americans have fallen for this scam. Who in America hasn't heard at least a thousand times, the worn-out line, *"this conspiracy theory has been debunked"*? But, has anyone ever heard this hypnotic mantra when it was followed by at least a two-minute synopsis of the ways in which the so-called conspiracy theory was *actually* debunked? I never have, and I don't think anyone else has either. *This is how mind control and social engineering work.*

In addition to the media that daily feeds us lies, we now also have fact-checkers, most of whom are professional liars as well. They are essentially nothing more than globalist fronts, designed to authenticate and reinforce the lies we've already been fed. The way this particular scam works is that they will tell the truth about a host of non-essential issues in order to gain credibility, and having accomplished that, they will then lie like the devil about the essential ones. Very predictably, they never, ever contradict the official government narrative about anything. There are a multitude of such disinformation services and channels all over the internet. It's a very simple way to brainwash an entire nation.

The question we might ask is why do we even need fact-checkers? Doesn't their very existence and popularity imply that many people are too lazy to do any research or thinking themselves? The truth has always been a rare commodity in this world. Looking for it is like looking for a diamond in a pile of rocks, and the only way to find it is to exert some effort. At the very least, it takes more effort than asking a few questions of some fact-checker. The bottom line is that lies come a dime a dozen, but truth is never cheap. A sign I saw in a mechanic shop summed this up perfectly. It talked about quality, but it works just as well for truth. *Quality/ Truth – Is Like Buying Oats. If you want nice, clean oats, you must pay a fair price. If however, you can be satisfied with oats that have already been through a horse – that comes a little cheaper.* Way too many people seem to be satisfied with cheap oats.

Hopefully, the next time you hear the terms "conspiracy theorist" or "conspiracy theory," you will no longer be fooled by them. Always remember that these are nothing more than hypnotic trigger words, specifically designed to shut down all critical thinking. Most of the time, their real meanings are: *Anyone who questions the official narrative of a particular issue, and anything the powers that be don't want us to know about!*

THE GLOBALIST CABAL

The globalist cabal has been with us for a very long time. From the time of Babel, it has been the desire of megalomaniacs to rule the world. But looking at history, we see that centralized power is the greatest of evils. One of the truest maxims ever uttered is that *"power tends to corrupt, and absolute power corrupts absolutely."* For some, it's the most intoxicating and addictive of all drugs, and it drives them stark-raving mad. Since 2020, we have seen with crystal clarity the kind of devastation it can cause.

Most people can't handle power, but many passionately desire it. Satan promises his followers riches, honor, and power. We know he's a liar, but if he never kept any of his promises, he soon wouldn't have any followers left. His most faithful followers get most of his goodies, and this is where the globalist cabal enters the picture. They already own just about everything on the planet, but they don't yet own it all, and that's breaking their greedy, little hearts. In addition to this, they don't yet have total control over every man, woman, and child, and that to them is simply unacceptable.

This Satanic gang has been around since Babel, influencing mankind from behind the scenes through a host of secret societies. What people should be asking, but few ever do, is why secret societies are secret. Way too many don't care, while many others believe they are meeting and operating in secret, because they love us and want to surprise us all with a pony. Apathy and naiveté are two of the most common human traits, and they have brought untold misery upon mankind.

I can't tell you about everything that goes on at the globalist cabal or secret society meetings, because they've never invited me. But that doesn't mean we are clueless about what these people are doing. Sometimes they tell us themselves, by giving us a sanitized version of their activities, and sometimes we get a much less sanitized version from defectors, researchers, and whistle-blowers. Perhaps the most prominent whistle-blower was one of our most beloved presidents, John F. Kennedy.

Before looking at what he had to say about this gang, let's look at a list of their most famous front organizations. One of the largest and perhaps most influential in America is the Council on Foreign Relations. This is a virtual Who's Who in the nation, and most people would be shocked if they knew how many prominent politicians are members. They are not just *in* the government, they practically *are* the government. They have many objectives, but their over-arching objective is to diminish America's sovereignty, in order to more easily assimilate it into a one-world superstate. CFR was founded in 1921, so they've had a long time to work toward all their objectives. Other prominent front organizations include the United Nations, the International Monetary Fund, the World Trade Organization, the Parliament of the World's Religions, the World Bank, the Trilateral Commission, the Club of Rome, the Bilderberg Group, the Committee of 300, as well the World Economic Forum, which predicted the Covid crisis, and which came up with the term "the Great Reset."

The globalist cabal owns, controls, or funds most institutes, foundations, think tanks, humanitarian organizations, civic groups, fraternal organizations, unions, medical associations, and religious groups. It would be difficult to find any large organization which they do not influence.

Most significantly, the cabal owns or controls all industries on the planet, which includes about 90% of all media outlets in America. Shaping public opinion is one of their top priorities, and they do so with TV channels, radio stations, newspapers, magazines, publishing houses, Hollywood studios, big tech companies, and social media platforms. In short, almost all media outlets with significant influence on public opinion are owned or controlled by the cabal. The greatest crimes that are being committed in the world are crimes we almost never hear about, because the greatest criminals are the ones who are informing us.

In order for their program to appear legitimate to the public, the cabal needs to control the four basic components of society. Commerce, academia, politics, and religion. The way the cabal accumulates and consolidates its power without raising public suspicion is in the following way: Commerce proposes ideas and changes that serve its interests and squeeze out small competitors. Academia then does studies and rubber stamps those proposals. They are then enacted into law, because they have the support of scientists, and are therefore needed to improve society. Religion then does its part, by telling the faithful that the changes are not just beneficial, but moral as well. The cabal has been controlling all four in America so long it's frightening. Our society is nothing like what most people imagine it to be.

Unlike most nations, America started with a Christian foundation. This has given many people the false impression that we are a Christian nation. It's true that concepts like inalienable rights and the separation of powers come from the Bible. In addition to this, approximately a third of our Constitution comes directly from Scripture. But unfortunately, the founding of our nation also had a dark element mixed in. That dark element can be found in numerous places, but the most prominent place is the back of a dollar bill.

The European Parliament building in Strasbourg, France is modeled after a famous painting of the unfinished tower of Babel. The unfinished pyramid on the back of a dollar bill is modeled after the same thing. This pyramid and the words below it are just a sliver of the evidence that the globalist cabal was present at America's founding. The words are *NOVUS ORDO SECLORUM,* which is Latin for *NEW WORLD ORDER.* In an effort to deflect and misdirect, the disinformation outlets tell us that those words can also be translated as *NEW ORDER OF THE AGES.* They're technically right, but why even bother telling us that when no globalist has ever used that term?

So, let's take a look at what some of the globalists and those who shill for them have said about their wonderful New World Order. Perhaps we can find out what kind of pony we're getting:

"For more than a century ideological extremists at either end of the political spectrum have seized upon well-publicized incidents such as my encounter with Castro to attack the Rockefeller family for the inordinate influence they claim we wield over American political and economic institutions. Some even believe we are part of a secret cabal

working against the best interests of the United States, characterizing my family and me as 'internationalists' and of conspiring with others around the world to build a more integrated global political and economic structure – one world, if you will. If that's the charge, I stand guilty, and I am proud of it." David Rockefeller, from his 2002 biography *Memoirs*

"We are grateful to The Washington Post, The New York Times, Time magazine and other great publications whose directors have attended our meetings and respected their promises of discretion for almost forty years"…. "It would have been impossible for us to develop our plan for the world if we had been subject to the bright lights of publicity during those years. But, the world is now much more sophisticated and prepared to march toward a world government. The supernational sovereignty of an intellectual elite and world bankers is surely preferable to the national auto-determination in past centuries." David Rockefeller, speaking at the June 1991 Bilderberg meeting in Baden Germany (a meeting also attended by Governor Bill Clinton, and Dan Quayle)

"The affirmative task before us is to create a New World Order." Vice-President Joe Biden, from speech at the Import Export Bank, April 5, 2013

"In the next century, nations as we know it will be obsolete; all states will recognize a single, global authority. National sovereignty wasn't such a great idea after all." Strobe Talbot, Deputy Secretary of State, *TIME*, July 1992

"I think that his [Obama's] task will be to develop an overall strategy for America in this period, when really a New World Order can be created." Henry Kissinger, *CNBC*, 2008

"We are moving toward a New World Order, the world of communism. We shall never turn off that road." Mikhail Gorbachev, 1987

"Fundamental Bible-believing people do not have the right to indoctrinate their children in their religious beliefs because we, the state, are preparing them for the year 2000, when America will be part of a one-world global society and their children will not fit in." Peter Hoagland, Nebraska State Senator, radio interview, 1983

"I will merely repeat that we are at present working, discreetly but with all our might, to wrest this mysterious political force called sovereignty out of the clutches of the local national states of our world. And all the time we are denying with our lips what we are doing with our hands." Arnold J. Toynbee, from a speech before the Royal Institute of International Affairs in Copenhagen, June 1931

"To achieve world government, it is necessary to remove from the minds of men, their individualism, loyalty to family tradition, national patriotism, and religious dogmas." G. Brock Chisholm, former Director of UN World Health Organization

"No one will enter the New World Order unless he or she will make a pledge to worship Lucifer. No one will enter the New Age unless he will take a Luciferian Initiation." David Spangler, Director of Planetary Initiative, United Nations

"We shall have world government whether or not we like it. The only question is whether world government will be achieved by conquest or consent." James Paul Warburg, CFR member to the Senate Foreign Relations Committee, February 17, 1950

"Under the momentum of globalization, the world is opening up and at an astonishing speed. Old boundaries of culture, identity and even nationhood are falling." Tony Blair, former British Prime Minister, April 3, 2008

"The technotronic era involves the gradual appearance of a more controlled society. Such a society would be dominated by an elite, unrestrained by traditional values. Soon it will be possible to assert almost continuous surveillance over every citizen and maintain up-to-date complete files containing even the most personal information about the citizen. These files will be subject to instantaneous retrieval by the authorities." Zbigniew Brzezinski, National Security Advisor

"The New World Order under the UN will reduce everything to one common denominator. The system will be made up of a single currency, single centrally financed government, single tax system, single language, single political system, single world court of justice, single state religion. Each person will have a registered number, without which he will not be allowed to buy or sell; and there will be one universal world church. Anyone who refuses to take part in the universal system will have no right to exist." Dr. Kurk E. Koch

"The United Nations can help bring about a new day....a new world order, and a long era of peace." President George H. W. Bush, from a speech to the General Assembly of the United Nations, October 1, 1990

"Give me control of a nation's money and I care not who makes the laws." Mayer Amschel Rothschild (1744 – 1812)

"We are on the verge of a global transformation. All we need is the right major crisis and the nations will accept the New World Order." David Rockefeller

The term New World Order has come to have a negative connotation, so in recent years, most globalists have chosen not to use it. Their latest favorite term is the Great Reset. Just like a chameleon, the globalist cabal adapts to different environments, and tries to sell their poison to the people under different names. If some of the following quotes seem like utter gibberish, it's because that's exactly what it is. The inane phrases and meaningless platitudes were deliberately designed to be unintelligible, so that the poison would be more palatable to an unsuspecting public. If the globalists flat out stated that the Great Reset simply means they'll be our absolute masters and we'll be their slaves, I suspect this probably wouldn't sit well with most people:

"This is the time for a Great Reset." Al Gore

"We must build more equal, inclusive and sustainable economies and societies that are more resilient in the face of pandemics, climate

change and the many other global changes we face."....."The Great Reset is a welcome recognition that this human tragedy must be a wake-up call."...."It is imperative that we re-imagine, rebuild, redesign, re-invigorate and re-balance our world." Antonio Guterres, Secretary General, United Nations

"This is a big moment. The World Economic Forum....is really going to have to play a front and center role in refining the Great Reset to deal with climate change and inequity – all of which is being laid bare as a consequence of COVID-19." John Kerry

"This global pandemic has demonstrated again how interconnected we are. We have to restore a functioning system of smart global cooperation structured to address the challenges of the next 50 years. The Great Reset will require us to integrate all stakeholders of global society into a community of common interest, purpose and action. We need a change of mindset, moving from short-term to long-term thinking, moving from shareholder capitalism to stakeholder responsibility. Environmental, social and good governance have to be a measured part of corporate and governmental accountability."..."The pandemic represents a rare but narrow window of opportunity to reflect, re-imagine and reset our world." Klaus Schwab, Executive Chairman of the World Economic Forum

"We have a unique but rapidly shrinking window of opportunity to learn lessons and reset ourselves on a more sustainable path."... *"We have a golden opportunity to seize something good from this [COVID-19] crisis. Its unprecedented shock-waves may well make people more receptive to big visions of change."* Prince Charles

"Now is the time to think what history would say about this crisis and now is the time for all of us to define our own role.".... *"What is it that would make it so that history would look at this crisis as the great opportunity for reset?"* Kristalina Georgieva, Managing Director of the International Monetary Fund

"OUR WORLD HAS CHANGED. OUR CHALLENGES ARE GREATER. OUR FRAGILITIES EXPOSED. OUR SYSTEMS NEED A RESET. EVERYONE HAS A ROLE TO PLAY. THE GREAT RESET. JOIN US." Promotional video for the Great Reset from the World Economic Forum

"YOU'LL OWN NOTHING AND YOU'LL BE HAPPY." As difficult as it may be to believe, this is the slogan the globalists chose for their Great Reset. The only thing they forgot to add is: *"WE'LL OWN EVERYTHING AND WE'LL BE HAPPIER."*

The preceding is just a tiny sampling of the globalist promotion of world governance. In the following section, we'll look at the warnings of a few individuals who saw behind the veil. This will give us a better insight into the activities, methods, and objectives of the globalist cabal. Some of these individuals were themselves used as pawns, and had only a fleeting glimpse of what was actually going on. Please notice how far back into America's history this darkness goes:

"The very word 'secrecy' is repugnant in a free and open society; and we are as a people inherently and historically opposed to secret societies, to secret oaths and to secret proceedings.".... *"For we are*

opposed around the world by a monolithic and ruthless conspiracy that relies primarily on covet means for expanding its sphere of influence, on infiltration instead of invasion, on subversion instead of elections, on intimidation instead of free choice, on guerrillas by night instead of armies by day. It is a system which has conscripted vast human and material resources into the building of a tightly knit, highly efficient machine that combines military, diplomatic, intelligence, economic, scientific and political operations. Its preparations are concealed, not published. Its mistakes are buried, not headlined. Its dissenters are silenced, not praised. No expenditure is questioned, no rumor is printed, no secret is revealed." President John F. Kennedy, April 27, 1961

"The drive of the Rockefellers and their allies is to create a one-world government combining super-capitalism and communism under the same tent, all under their control."…. "Do I mean conspiracy? Yes I do. I am convinced there is such a plot, international in scope, generations old in planning, and incredibly evil in intent." Congressman Larry P. McDonald, 1976 (killed in the 1983 Korean Airlines 747 flight that was shot down by the Soviets)

"The most powerful clique in these elitist groups have one objective in common… they want to bring about the surrender of the sovereignty of the national independence of the United States. A second clique of international members in the CFR… comprises the Wall Street international bankers and their key agents. Primarily, they want the world-banking monopoly from whatever power ends up in the control of global government."… "The main purpose of the Council on Foreign Relations is promoting the disarmament of U.S. sovereignty

and independence and submergence into an all-powerful, one world government." Rear Admiral Chester Ward, 16-year member of the CFR

"The CFR, dedicated to one-world government, financed by a number of the largest tax-exempt foundations, and wielding such power and influence over our lives in the areas of finance, business, labor, military, education and mass communication media, should be familiar to every American concerned with good government and with preserving and defending the U.S. Constitution and our free-enterprise system. Yet, the nation's right to know machinery — the news media — usually so aggressive in exposures to inform people, remain conspicuously silent when it comes to the CFR, its members and their activities....The CFR is the establishment. Not only does it have influence and power in key decision-making positions at the highest levels of government to apply pressure from above, but it also finances and uses individuals and groups to bring pressure from below, to justify the high-level decisions for converting the United States from a sovereign constitutional republic into a servile member of a one-world dictatorship." Congressman John R. Rarick, 1971

"In my view the Trilateral Commission represents a skillful, coordinated effort to seize control and consolidate the four centers of power — political, monetary, intellectual and ecclesiastical. What the Trilaterals truly intend is the creation of a worldwide economic power superior to the political governments of the nation-states involved."... "As managers and creators of the system they will rule the future." Senator Barry Goldwater, from his book *With No Apologies*

"The real menace of our Republic is the invisible government, which like a giant octopus sprawls its slimy legs over our cities, states and nation. To depart from mere generalizations, let me say that at the head of this octopus are the Rockefeller-Standard Oil interests and a small group of powerful banking houses generally referred to as the international bankers. The little coterie of powerful international bankers virtually run the United States government for their own selfish purposes. They practically control both political parties, write political platforms, make catspaws of party leaders, use the leading men of private organizations, and resort to every device to place in nomination for high public office only such candidates as will be amenable to the dictates of corrupt big business." Francis Hylan, NYC Mayor, 1922

"The modern banking system manufactures money out of nothing. The process is perhaps the most astounding piece of sleight of hand that was ever invented. Banking was conceived in inequity and born in sin. Bankers own the earth. Take it away from them but leave them the power to create money, and with a flick of a pen, they will create enough money to buy it back again. Take this great power away from them and all great fortunes like mine will disappear, for then this would be a better and happier world to live in. But if you want to continue to be slaves of bankers and pay the cost of your own slavery, then let bankers continue to create money and control credit." Josiah Stamp, President of the Rothschild Bank of England, and the second richest man in Britain in the 1920's, speaking at the University of Texas in 1927

"History records that the money changers have used every form of abuse, intrigue, deceit, and violent means possible to maintain

their control over governments by controlling money and its issuance President James Madison

"The real truth of the matter is, as you and I know, that a financial element in the large centers has owned the government of the U.S. since the days of Andrew Jackson." President Franklin D. Roosevelt

"For a long time I felt that FDR had developed many thoughts and ideas that were his own to benefit this country, the United States. But he didn't. Most of his thoughts, his political ammunition, as it were, were carefully manufactured for him in advance by the Council on Foreign Relations – One World Money group. Brilliantly, with great gusto, like a fine piece of artillery, he exploded that prepared 'ammunition' in the middle of an unsuspecting target, the American people, and thus paid off and returned his internationalist political support." Curtis B. Dall, FDR's son-in-law from his book *My Exploited Father-in-Law*

"The real rulers in Washington are invisible, and exercise power from behind the scenes." Felix Frankfurter, Supreme Court Justice, 1952

"Some of the biggest men in the United States, in the field of commerce and manufacture, are afraid of somebody, are afraid of something. They know that there is a power somewhere so organized, so subtle, so watchful, so interlocked, so complete, so pervasive, that they had better not speak above their breath when they speak in condemnation of it."…. "I am a most unhappy man. I have unwittingly ruined my country. A great industrial nation is controlled by its system

of credit. Our system of credit is concentrated. The growth of the nation, therefore, and all our activities are in the hands of a few men. We have come to be one of the worst ruled, one of the most completely controlled and dominated Governments in the civilized world. We are no longer a Government by free opinion, no longer a Government by conviction and the vote of the majority, but a Government by the opinion and duress of a small group of dominant men." President Woodrow Wilson

"It is well enough that people of the nation do not understand our banking and monetary system, for if they did, I believe there would be a revolution before tomorrow morning." Henry Ford, founder of the Ford Motor Company

"Mr. Chairman, we have in this Country one of the most corrupt institutions the world has ever known. I refer to the Federal Reserve Board and the Federal Reserve Banks, hereinafter called the Fed. The Fed has cheated the Government of these United States and the people of the United States out of enough money to pay the Nation's debt. The depredations and iniquities of the Fed has cost enough money to pay the National debt several times over." Congressman Louis T. McFadden

"Whoever controls the volume of money in our country is absolute master of all industry and commerce....when you realize that the entire system is very easily controlled, one way or another, by a few powerful men at the top, you will not have to be told how periods of inflation and depression originate." President James A. Garfield

"The money powers prey upon the nation in times of peace and conspire against it in times of adversity. The banking powers are more despotic than a monarchy, more insolent than autocracy, more selfish than bureaucracy. They denounce as public enemies all who question their methods or throw light upon their crimes. I have two great enemies, the Southern army in front of me and the bankers in the rear. Of the two, the one at my rear is my greatest foe. Corporations have been enthroned, and an era of corruption in high places will follow. The money power of the country will endeavor to prolong its reign by working upon the prejudices of the people until the wealth is aggregated in the hands of a few, and the Republic is destroyed."
President Abraham Lincoln

"If the people only understood the rank injustice of our money and banking system, there would be a revolution before morning."
President Andrew Jackson

Perhaps you're beginning to see that the globalists possess an insatiable lust for money and power. In many ways, they are like the rich, corrupt uncle who everyone in the family kisses up to, so that he will remember them in his will. The history of America and the world at large, is a story about a great number of people kissing up to their rich uncle, knowing full well that he is a scoundrel, and in the process becoming just like him. By themselves, the globalists could accomplish very little, but through their wealth, they've managed to corrupt multitudes to do their bidding. A few presidents and many others have tried to warn the American people about this godless gang. Their warnings generally fell on deaf ears, and some of them paid the ultimate price.

The New World Order is not new at all. The rich robbing the poor and the strong abusing the weak is the order that's always been around. The only difference is that those who benefit from this arrangement would now like to make it global.

Most people have heard the proverbial story of the frog and the boiling pot of water. Drop a frog into a boiling pot and it will immediately jump out. But drop the frog into a pot containing cool water and slowly turn up the heat, and the frog won't notice the danger until it's too late. In the next few chapters, we'll look at how the globalist cabal has been *incrementally* preparing the American people for the chaos and madness that they unleashed on our country in 2020.

STAGED EVENTS OF THE PAST

History is full of events staged by the ruling class that most people then living wholeheartedly embraced as real. Perhaps the most popular type of staged event is when rulers attack their own countries, and blame it on whoever they wish to go to war with. This is known as a "false flag" attack, and countless men and women have thrown away their lives, fighting wars based on lies. In this chapter, we'll look at just two staged events out of many that most Americans have embraced as real.

The Word of God tells us that all which is hidden will eventually be brought to light, but many staged events stay hidden for long periods of time. The reason this is so often the case, is because of a universal human blind spot. It is the peculiar notion that our own tribe, nation or ethnic group is superior in moral character to all others. For example, Americans have no problem comprehending how Germany could have produced a Hitler and Russia a Stalin, and how those nations were then deceived by these two despots. They were Germans and Russians after all. But most of our fellow citizens don't believe such a thing could ever happen to us, *because we are Americans!* This kind of thinking is not only naive but dangerous, because the Word of God also tells us that pride goes before a fall. *The very reason there was a Hitler and a Stalin was because of an excessive amount of national pride!*

For those who've made idols of our leaders and our government, the next few paragraphs won't be pleasant. But lies are a deadly disease, and they *always* destroy. The truth on the other hand, while often unpleasant, *always* heals.

If anyone, other than God, had prior knowledge of an event, that would be conclusive and indisputable proof that the event was staged. The attacks of 9/11 and the London bombings fall into this category. Please consider the following two quotes:

"Out of these troubled times, our fifth objective, a new world order can emerge." George H. W. Bush, from a speech before a joint session of Congress, September 11, 1990

"What is at stake is more than one small country. It is a big idea, a new world order, where diverse nations are drawn together in common cause to achieve the universal aspirations of mankind; peace and security, freedom and the rule of law. Such is a world worthy of our struggle and worthy of our children's future." George H. W. Bush, from a speech before a joint session of Congress, September 11, 1991

As we all know, September 11, 2001, America was attacked. The dates of the two speeches by former President Bush are clear evidence of prior knowledge by someone in our government, but that's just the beginning. September 11, 2001 was also one of the busiest peacetime days in the entire history of America's military. That day, the Defense Department was running more than half a dozen war game exercises and airline hijacking simulations. One of them was *Northern Vigilance*, in which a significant number of fighter aircraft were diverted to Canada and Alaska to participate in mock hijack exercises. *Vigilant Warrior* was another live fly exercise. *Vigilant Guardian* was a command center hijack exercise, in which false blips were inserted onto radar screens in the *northeast* part of the country. This of course caused massive confusion among air traffic controllers, who sometimes had to deal with more than two dozen possible hijackings. These exercises and others ensured that our national defense would be *anything but vigilant*, on the very day America was attacked.

This is conclusive and undeniable evidence of prior knowledge, but if anyone thinks it's all just a huge set of coincidences, I'd like to point out that what I've shared is only the tip of the iceberg. Scores of books and documentaries have been produced, which provide a thousand times more evidence than this that the attacks of 9/11 were a staged event. Not only circumstantial evidence, but also an astounding amount of physical evidence. Those who read one book or watch one documentary, wonder afterward why all Americans don't know this yet. The answer is quite simple. *The professional liars made sure that most Americans would never read one book or watch one documentary about what really happened on 9/11!* They told the nation a bedtime story about terrorists in caves, and like little children, most Americans simply closed their eyes and drifted off to sleep.

The second staged event were the London bombings that took place on July 7, 2005. This one was also made to look like the work of Islamic terrorists. Minutes before the simultaneous bombings occurred, a crisis management firm by the name of Visor

Consultants was conducting a simulation exercise of a terrorist attack on London's transportation system. The underground subway trains chosen for the exercise were the *same trains, at the same locations, and they were mock attacked at almost the same minute as those that were attacked for real!* The managing director of Visor Consultants, Peter Power, appeared on BBC television shortly after the attacks and said that the coincidence made his hair stand on end.

That is some kind of coincidence! It has been calculated that the probability of this simulation exercise coinciding with the actual attacks randomly in a ten-year period is one chance in:

3,715,592,613,265,750,000,000,000,000,000,000,000,000

But we don't really need this calculation, because everyone knows that such a coincidence is impossible. Even without the mountain of additional evidence, this alone proves that the London bombings were a staged event.

If one wishes to know how an event was staged, who was behind it, and what their objectives were, one must read some books or watch some documentaries. But the ultimate proof that an event was staged is *prior knowledge.*

In regard to 9/11, I wish to add some comments. Many influential truth tellers who expose evil and corruption in our society, nevertheless give credence to the official narrative of this particular event. This seems more than strange, because the evidence that 9/11 was a staged event is so overwhelming, it can't be denied. So, why would people who tell the truth about a host of issues endorse such a monstrous lie? I can think of only two possibilities. The first possibility is that those who routinely research everything meticulously, did zero research into this issue, and unquestioningly accepted what was dished out by the media that they continually accuse of lying. The second possibility, which seems much more likely, is that they know the truth, but are afraid to touch it with a ten-foot pole. A sacred mythology has grown up around this issue, and perhaps they feel that if they question this mythology in any way, they'll lose their credibility on other issues. Whichever is true about these people, the end result is that the nation remains in the dark about one of the greatest deceptions of our time.

What makes this particular deception so insidious is its appeal to patriotism. Those who question the sacred mythology are often accused of being unpatriotic, and most people don't want such a charge leveled against them. I suspect that this is the main reason that many who are otherwise truth tellers, deliberately endorse this deception. They can't understand why we've been losing the culture war, so I'll clue them in. Many of the lies permeating our society are based on much bigger lies, and unless those are exposed, they can forget about ever winning the culture war. It is the height of presumption and folly for people to think that they can invoke the name of a holy God in this war and receive His blessing, while they themselves are knowingly lying!

The official 9/11 narrative *cannot* be factually supported. Anyone who has done the slightest bit of research knows this. It has cost the American people dearly in money, blood, the loss of civil liberties, and the loss of international prestige. Yet despite all of this, many Americans cling to this deception like a life preserver. The only explanation for this is massive mind control.

It's the most potent weapon the globalists employ, to get the vast majority of people to dance to their tune and to march willingly to their own destruction. In the next chapter, we'll take a brief look at the greatest mind control tool ever invented. This invention allows the globalists to essentially commit their crimes in broad daylight, and to cover them up at the same time. Without this invention, the horrendous climax of history, which is outlined for us in the book of Revelation, would not be possible.

A PRODUCT BEING MANUFACTURED IN OUR LIVING ROOMS

Throughout most of history, the globalists feared the idea of the masses being educated. But about two centuries ago, it dawned on them that education could be one of their greatest tools for achieving their ends. In America and wherever else their influence reached, they began making education for children compulsory, and with that move, they hit the mother lode. Under the guise of freeing people from ignorance, they have actually been able to increase their level of ignorance, because possessing very little accurate information is much closer to the truth than possessing a great deal of false information. By controlling and manipulating the curriculum, the globalists have succeeded in brainwashing generation after generation.

The education of children in the early days of our Republic was generally relegated to one-room schoolhouses, and it was voluntary. It mostly focused on Biblical morality and what became known as the three R's; reading, writing, and arithmetic. A secondary focus was on history and science. After a six-year education, most students had a fairly accurate understanding of the world and could read and write. That began to change in the 1850's, when states started making school attendance compulsory. By 1918, every child in America had to attend school, and it has been a downward slide ever since.

As our culture changed, more and more Socialists, atheists, pagans, and God-haters gained influential positions in the compulsory public education system. Today, about a hundred years later, they control it completely, and that makes things for the globalists much, much easier. Biblical morality has gradually been completely removed and has been replaced by cultural morality. Subjects taught now are evolution, humanism, socialism, sociology, psychology, diversity and tolerance, as well new forms of sexual deviancy. Most of today's educators consider these much more important than the three R's. As far as history is concerned, *real* history has been replaced by what is known as *revisionist* history, which is essentially leftist propaganda. It's no surprise therefore that even though America spends more money per student ($16,000 yearly) than all nations, it ranks 26th in academic achievement out of 65 nations.

American public schools have been specifically designed to teach children what to think, rather than how to think, and today they are little more than indoctrination camps for the recruitment of mindless, godless, subservient robots. The three basic lessons which are pounded into children's heads more than any other are: *There is no God, never question authority, and always obey.* After 12 years of this systematic brainwashing, even the 20% of High School graduates who've learned virtually nothing and are functionally illiterate, have mastered these three basic lessons. They may not be able to spell the word "mask," but they'll wear one for months or years if someone in authority tells them to, and they won't take it off until someone in authority gives them permission. *They're precisely the kind of citizens a corrupt government wants and needs.*

In the early part of the 20th century, a society that was already being systematically brainwashed, witnessed the arrival of the greatest mind control and propaganda tool ever invented. A talking box with pictures that we've come to know as television. It was a dream come true for those with a need for endless, mindless entertainment, as well as for dictators. In combination with the dismal education system, the television has been the primary instrument for gradually turning America into a godless police state.

The cultural transformation of "One Nation Under God" into a pagan one was well underway a hundred years ago. Because of compulsory public education and the invention of television, that transformation was much faster than most people realize. The first talking boxes began appearing in people's homes in the 1930's, and in 1966, *Time* magazine asked whether God is dead on its front-page cover. There wasn't much of a backlash against the magazine, because by that time, a great number of Americans were asking the same question. *If God wasn't really dead, then many wished He was.*

Emboldened by the huge cultural shift of the 1960's which they engineered, the globalists cranked up the anti-God, pro-government propaganda to new levels. They began to push a host of strange agendas and the boundaries of decency. Their primary tool for reshaping the culture was the talking box. By the 1970's, practically everyone in America had a talking box, and the social engineering and mind control became much easier. The box began to be viewed as the arbiter of all truth and gained cult status. Walter Cronkite ended his nightly newscast with the words *"that's the way it is,"* and most people gradually came to believe that if the box said it, it must be true. Conversely, they came to believe that if the box didn't say it, it couldn't possibly be true. Former President Richard Nixon summed it up best when he said, *"the American people don't believe anything until they see it on television."* It never occurred to most Americans that they were being subtly manipulated and indoctrinated, by a tiny group of God-hating, Satan-worshiping megalomaniacs.

Long before the arrival of the talking box, dictators, hypnotists, and hustlers understood the power of words. They also understood that this power could be magnified by repetition. It's no wonder then that this technique has been adopted by the owners of the mainstream media. They have a host of agendas that they are continually shoving down the throats of the public, and even the most nonsensical ones begin to seem reasonable after thousands of repetitions. To give even more credibility to their agendas, they use celebrities, sports heroes, "experts," and anyone else who can be bought to shill for them.

When carefully analyzed, three things lie at the core of all their agendas. *The destruction of all personal rights and freedoms, the destruction of Christianity, and the destruction of America.* Here's a list of just a few: The anti-God agenda, the pro-abortion agenda, the LGBTQ+ agenda, the green agenda, the climate-change agenda, the depopulation agenda, the social justice agenda, the bigger government agenda, the gun-control agenda, the America is racist agenda, the hate-speech agenda, the war on drugs agenda, the anti-smoking agenda, the pro-vaccine agenda, the mask agenda, the pro-evolution agenda, the euthanasia agenda, the Feminist agenda, and the list goes on and on. The next time you turn on the TV news, please notice how much of what is being presented is news, and how much is agenda propaganda. One Fox News Channel slogan we used to hear often is that they report and we decide, but that slogan is decades out of date. Today, the slogan for every single mainstream TV news outlet in America should be: *"We Decide For You, Because You're Too Stupid To Decide For Yourself."* In fairness, it should be noted that Fox *does* allow its viewers some measure of independent thought, whereas outlets like CNN and MSNBC allow their viewers absolutely none.

What most people are not aware of is that viewing television puts a person into an altered state of consciousness. The human brain has four wave patterns. Delta occurs in deep sleep and Theta in light sleep. Beta occurs when engaged in critical, logical thinking, which happens when we read a book, or do anything that requires concentration. The last one is Alpha, which is a hypnotic state that occurs when viewing television, or when engaged in anything else that doesn't require concentration. Within a minute of seeing the first image on the TV screen, we fall into a hypnotic trance and our minds become highly suggestible to all input. This is enhanced by the flicker rate of the television, which was designed to coincide exactly with the rate of our Alpha brain waves. *The effect of this is the same as when a hypnotist waves an object before someone's eyes, and the end result is whatever programming the hypnotist wants it to be!* There really *is* a product being manufactured in our living rooms, and that product of course is *us!*

All people believe themselves to be independent thinkers, but because we all grew up in the era of the talking box cult, very few actually are. Those who are still in the cult believe various things, but most of them don't have a clue why. You can tell who these people are, because when discussing any issue with them, the most you will ever get from them is some TV phrases or slogans. It becomes apparent quite quickly that they've never given the issue any thought at all. Another way to tell that someone is a member of the cult is that they tend to get very upset if the teaching of the box is ever questioned. *The first and most important commandment of the talking box cult is that the box is always right!*

Christians are often mocked for their simple faith in the Bible, which is best summed up by the old bumper sticker *"God Said It, I Believe It, That Settles It."* I therefore find it ironic and amusing that most of those doing the mocking, live by the motto *"The Box Said It, I Believe It, That Settles It."*

There's no escaping the sad fact that most people today, think like the box, talk like the box, and do most of what the box tells them to do. When reading the book of Revelation years ago, I used to wonder how two smooth talking snake-oil salesmen could compel most people in the world to be branded like cattle with some disgusting mark. But after witnessing the awesome, hypnotic power of the talking box since 2020, there's no mystery about it at all!

EVENT 201 DRESS REHEARSAL FOR A PANDEMIC

I believe we can all agree that prior knowledge of an event is proof that the event has been staged. The first hint that a "pandemic" was in the works comes from a 2010 Rockefeller Foundation document. It's entitled *"Scenarios for the Future of Technology and International Development,"* and it lays out four possible future scenarios for the world. The four are: *"Clever Together," "Hack Attack," "Smart Scramble,"* and *"Lock Step."*

Clever Together envisions *"a world in which highly coordinated and successful strategies emerge for addressing both urgent and entrenched worldwide issues."* Hack Attack envisions *"an economically unstable and shock-prone world in which governments weaken, criminals thrive, and dangerous innovations emerge."* Smart Scramble envisions *"an economically depressed world in which individuals and communities develop localized, makeshift solutions to a growing set of problems."* Lock Step envisions *"a world of tighter top-down government control and more authoritarian leadership, with limited innovation and growing citizen pushback."*

Knowing what we already know about the globalists, which of these four scenarios would they be most likely to choose if they were preparing to stage an event? I don't know about you, but I'd go with Lock Step.

The Lock Step scenario takes up eight pages of the document, but I'll just share the highlights: *"The pandemic that the world had been anticipating for years finally hit. Unlike 2009's H1N1, this new influenza strain – originating from wild geese – was extremely virulent and deadly. Even the most pandemic-prepared nations were quickly overwhelmed when the virus streaked around the world, infecting nearly 20 percent of the global population and killing 8 million in just seven months, the majority of them healthy young adults. The pandemic also had a deadly effect on economies: international mobility of both people and goods screeched to a halt, debilitating industries like tourism and breaking global supply chains. Even locally, normally bustling shops and office buildings sat empty for months, devoid of both employees and costumers"*…. *"During the pandemic, national leaders around the world flexed their authority and imposed airtight rules and restrictions, from the mandatory wearing of face masks to body-temperature checks at the entries to communal spaces like train stations and supermarkets. Even after the pandemic faded, this more authoritarian control and oversight of citizens and their activities stuck and even intensified"*…. *"At first, the notion of a more controlled world gained wide acceptance and approval. Citizens willingly gave up some of their sovereignty – and their privacy – to more paternalistic states in exchange for greater safety and stability. Citizens were more tolerant, and even eager, for top-down direction and oversight, and national leaders had more latitude to impose order in the ways they saw fit"*…. *"By 2025, people seemed to be growing weary of so much top down control and letting leaders and authorities make choices for them. Wherever national interests clashed with individual interests, there was conflict. Sporadic pushback became increasingly organized and coordinated, as disaffected youth and people who had seen their status and opportunities slip away – largely in developing countries – incited civil unrest."*

After reading that, do you get the idea that the globalists are master psychologists, and that they know us better than we know ourselves? I know that it's unimaginable to the average person that some cabal somewhere would be plotting and scheming behind closed doors to take over the world and to enslave humanity. Most people believe that the globalist elites are just going about their business, the same as everyone else. What most people fail to understand however, is that plotting and scheming to achieve total world domination *is* their business! It has been their business for centuries, and after what they've unleashed on the world in 2020, they're almost there.

The Lock Step scenario may be disturbing, but it's just an introduction to Event 201. On October 18, 2019, John Hopkins Center for Health Security, in partnership with the World Economic Forum and the Bill and Melinda Gates Foundation, conducted a pandemic response exercise in New York City. Event 201 was an exercise based on a fictional virus pandemic that would eventually kill 65 million people. Among the participants were representatives from the United Nations, as well as leaders from the world of business, public health, government, and the media.

The panelists were presented with the scenario of a virus which spread from pigs to humans, and which caused a worldwide pandemic. They were then charged with the task of containing the spread and dealing with all related issues. Topics covered were the economic fallout, bailouts, supply chain problems, vaccines, travel bans, and other restrictions. One of the restrictions discussed was the censorship of alternative viewpoints, including criminal punishment for spreading misinformation about the pandemic. Possible internet shutdowns to stop the spread of misinformation were also discussed. But perhaps the creepiest panel discussion involved *recruitment of faith leaders and faith-based organizations to lend credibility to the official narrative.* When the first case of Corona virus appeared in Wuhan, China eight weeks later, *the exact scenario they were play-acting began to play out for real!* Can anyone guess which type of virus was chosen for the pandemic exercise? You guessed it, *Corona virus!*

Hollywood has been spinning fairy tales of superheroes with superpowers, and blurring the lines between fantasy and reality for a very long time. So long in fact, that today many people can't tell what's real and what's not, what's possible and what's not. I would suggest that to be able to foretell the future with the uncanny accuracy we've just seen is *categorically impossible!* Yet, the globalists seem to be able do it time after time. Those who need an extra nudge to confront some very uncomfortable truths, may wish to ponder the words of Doctor Anthony Fauci, which he uttered January 10, 2017, ten days before Donald Trump's inauguration: *"There is no question that there will be a challenge to the coming administration in the arena of infectious diseases"…. "There will be a surprise outbreak."* Some people may finally be ready to start asking some serious questions, and perhaps the first question could be: *How could Dr. Fauci possibly have known?*

A YEAR OF STAGED EVENTS AND PSYCHOLOGICAL OPERATIONS

I became aware that something very unnatural was happening in February of 2020. There seemed to be an inordinate amount of time being spent by the mainstream media on a relatively minor story. Yes, there had been some kind of disease outbreak in China, but there have been much bigger outbreaks in the past that have never gained international attention. Some of those outbreaks numbered in *tens of thousands of fatalities,* and weren't even mentioned by our media. The Corona virus became the number one story by February, although at that time there weren't even *three thousand fatalities in China!* It was more than suspicious, it was downright bizarre.

By March, it became clear as day that we were in the middle of a staged event. The mainstream news outlets were beginning to devote more and more time to the "pandemic," and by the middle of the month, that was the *only* story being covered. *It was 24/7 coverage of a disease, which at that time had taken about 100 American lives!* Because of the horrendous devastation Covid-19 was causing, the nation needed to go into a lockdown. Fox News Channel quickly produced a pandemic special and was heavily promoting it. The promo mentioned the major disease outbreaks of the last century, including the 1918 Spanish Influenza outbreak, which had taken at least 50 million lives. It ended with the announcer stating that nothing like Covid had ever come our way. With about 100 deaths in America, Fox was essentially telling its viewers that Covid was more deadly than the 1918 virus! What more could our friends at Fox have done to let everyone know that this was all a show? But the talking box said it was real, so naturally almost everyone believed it was real.

One after another, inconsistencies, contradictions, nonsense, and utter absurdities began to pile up, and today they're about a mile high. Some of the absurdities were obviously deliberate, and these are what we might call mind games or psychological operations. Such operations are designed to twist people's minds into pretzels, until a significant segment of the population can't tell up from down.

In early March, Dr. Fauci told the nation in a *60 Minutes* interview that *"there's no reason to be walking around with a mask."* He explained that wearing masks might make people feel a little bit better and provide an illusion of protection, but that they don't provide the kind of protection people think they do. A month later, wearing masks became the official recommendation, and few weeks later, a mandate. I suppose this development came about as a result of *"following the science"* that we've all heard so much about. But isn't someone who's been in the health care field for decades already familiar with the standard protocols for masks? In July, Dr. Fauci recommended wearing goggles, and as ridiculous as this recommendation might seem to anyone who's sane, it does actually make sense in a perverted kind of way. Since a hypothetical airborne virus particle can infect a person through the eyes as it might through the mouth or nose, wearing a mask alone is obviously useless. So, what was the point of mask mandates? This falls into the category of an absurdity or a psychological operation.

We will deal with the issue of masks and their effectiveness in a later chapter, but assuming masks work, why social distance? If social distancing works, why wear masks? And if both work, why the need for all those plastic barriers that appeared all across the country virtually overnight? The sudden appearance of the plastic barriers was a huge red flag, which should have alerted everyone that we were being played. Please consider the fact that these barriers were everywhere within two weeks of the lockdown. One explanation is that they were all beamed down from the Starship Enterprise. The only other explanation I can think of is that they were sitting in warehouses, waiting to be shipped! For those with math skills, I have a relatively simple math question. Assuming a dozen average-sized factories were retooled to manufacture these plastic barriers for every place of business in the country, how many *years* would it take to make them all?

This is just the beginning of the absurdities that the American people have been subjected to since the early part of 2020. Please consider the commercials that began airing a few days after the lockdown. It normally takes about six months to produce a commercial, but the "pandemic" commercials appeared virtually overnight, the same as the plastic barriers. Perhaps they put a rush on them, but there was something extremely unusual about these particular commercials. Representing most major companies, they were virtually identical, including background music! To get the full impact of the sameness of all these commercials, one needs to see and hear them side by side. Someone took the time to produce a short compilation, and it is worth watching. After watching it, you should have no problem seeing the scam that has been worked upon the nation and the world. The video is entitled *This Video Will Wake Up Even The Dumbest Of Sheeple.* In it, you will also see a compilation of clips from local TV affiliates around the country, in which the anchors are reading from a script that is word for word identical! It's a great visual example of what propaganda and mind control look like.

On March 13, 2020, when there were fewer than 120 fatalities, President Trump declared a state of national emergency. There was talk that millions would die. But by that time, the virus had pretty much run its course in China, and the death toll there was less than 4,000. As of December 30, 2020, the death toll in China was 4,634. At the same time, the Department of Health and Human Services came out with a 100-page report, which outlined a long-range plan for fighting the pandemic. The report declared that the crisis *"will last 18 months or longer,"* and that it could include *"multiple waves."* Senator Jack Reed, Democrat of Rhode Island, stated that *"the American public is on a wartime footing in terms of battling the spread of this disease, and the Pentagon has to be a part of the effort to help protect the health and safety of the American people."*

By the middle of April, about 300 million Americans were under some sort of lockdown. The President said he wanted to see the country open up by Easter, but the health "experts" insisted that was too soon. We heard them say that we first needed to *"flatten the curve,"* and that this might happen by the beginning of May. So, we waited anxiously for May, but to those who were paying attention, it was obvious that the country wouldn't be opening anytime soon. The curve *was* flattened, but when May came, the lockdown stayed in place. After that, the line on the graph kept going steadily down until it reached the valley, but the *"experts"* kept saying *"just two more weeks."* After weeks of being in the valley, when the virus was all but gone, the mask mandates went into effect!

Up until this point, the Covid show was something to behold. We had hospital ships that remained empty, tent hospitals that remained empty, and regular hospitals that were for the most part empty. Sometime around the beginning of April, a hospital in New York State started putting up tents in the parking lot, but when it came to light that the hospital was nearly empty, they were quickly taken down. Please bear in mind that America has over 5,500 hospitals, and that all this was going on when there were less than 1,000 fatalities! Similar shows were taking place in other countries, and bored hospital nurses from around the world began to expose the scam on social media.

We constantly heard that this or that person died, not *of Covid* or *from Covid,* but *after testing positive for Covid.* That strange terminology began to make sense when doctors from around the country started coming forward and blowing the whistle on a massive cause of death fraud that was taking place. They were being directed by the CDC to put Covid-19 on death certificates, *no matter what their patients died from.* The only thing that was necessary is that a person tested positive for Covid. So, people died from stage four cancer, heart disease, strokes, heart attacks, diabetes, tuberculosis, pneumonia, the flu, and every imaginable ailment, and many of those deaths suddenly became Covid deaths. It's difficult to keep a pandemic going if people aren't dying, so this was the simple solution. Dr. Scott Jensen, a prominent medical doctor in Minnesota who also served as a State Senator, was brought before the medical board and threatened with the revocation of his license. This happened because he spoke publicly about CDC directives to list Covid as the cause of death whenever anyone who tested positive died. Many other doctors who spoke publicly and exposed the scam were similarly threatened and harassed.

The reason so few people were dying of Covid was because it's apparently a very mild virus. When the statistics began to come in, it was discovered that about 80% of those who contract Covid don't have a single symptom, and that the average age of those who die from it is 78. The vast majority of the remaining 20% experience mild to moderate symptoms and quickly recover. The reality is nothing like the picture that has been painted for us.

Every aspect of the "pandemic" has been steeped in deception. For example, some people stood in long lines waiting for a Covid test and left before getting tested. While in line, they filled out a form that asked for their name and address. They were surprised to get a letter in the mail a few days later, notifying them that they tested positive. In Florida, it was discovered that in multiple labs processing Covid tests, 100% of the tests were positive. Such stories abounded.

But what does it even mean if a person tests positive? According to Dr. Kary Mullis, who was awarded a Nobel Prize in chemistry and who is the inventor of the PCR test, *absolutely nothing!* He has stated repeatedly that with the PCR test, it's possible to find almost anything in anybody. Kary Mullis had a long-standing controversy with Dr. Fauci for misusing his test, which he designed for research and forensic purposes, and *not for diagnosing a disease.* He boldly denounced Dr. Fauci and repeatedly challenged him to a debate. Here's what he had to say in one interview: *"Guys like Fauci get up there and start talking, you know, he doesn't know anything really about anything, and I'd say that to his face. Nothing. The man thinks you can take a blood sample and stick it in an electron microscope and if it's got a virus in there, you'll know it. He doesn't understand electron microscopy, and he doesn't understand medicine, and he should not be in the position like he's in. Most of those guys up there on the top are just total administrative people, and they don't know anything about what's going on at the bottom. You know, those guys have got an agenda, which is not what we would like them to have, being that we pay for them to take care of our health in some way. They've got a personal kind of agenda, they make up their own rules as they go, they change them when they want to. And Tony Fauci doesn't mind going on television in front of the people who pay his salary and lie directly into the camera."* When testing for Covid with a PCR test and you amplify the sample to less than 30 cycles, you will get no positives. If you amplify it to 60 cycles, every test will come back positive. To make the point and expose the scam, a papaya and a goat were tested, and the samples came back positive. Because of a meaningless test that can be so easily manipulated, the scammers were able to have as many positives as they needed at every stage of the Covid operation.

Months went by, and while the number of deaths were minimal, the number of cases skyrocketed. This was all the media talked about, but what they failed to mention was that every day more and more people were being tested. All of it created the illusion that Covid was out of control. It also gave the government a justification for continued lockdowns and restrictions.

We'll probably never know whether it was the work of a whistle-blower, or if the CDC simply made a mistake, but in late August of 2020, something very revealing showed up on the CDC website. It was the admission that of all the deaths attributed to Covid, only 6% were deaths without additional co-morbidities. In other words, 94% of those who supposedly died from Covid had serious pre-existing conditions, which likely caused their deaths. Each year, about 40 to 80 thousand people in America die from the seasonal flu, so if you do the calculations based on the CDC admission, you'll discover that Covid may not even be as deadly as the flu. This should have ended the hoax, but the professional liars got busy and smoothed that little fiasco over. A little bit of double talk from leading health "experts," and the public was back on board with the pandemic narrative. The smoothing over, which was laced with a lot of medical jargon to confuse the public, went something like this: Yes, the 94% did have other, very serious health conditions and were standing on the edge of a cliff, but Covid came along and knocked them off that cliff, so it was perfectly appropriate to list Covid as the cause of death. That means if someone had stage four cancer, and three months ago the doctors gave that patient two months to live, if that patient tested positive for Covid and died, it's clear as day that Covid killed him. A lot of people heard that and thought it made perfect medical sense, especially since it came from trusted health professionals like Dr. Fauci. The strangest thing of all is that those people didn't want it to be true that no pandemic existed. Quite the contrary. They were greatly relieved when Dr. Fauci and many others reassured them that it did. Never in my life have I seen anything close to the bizarre thinking and bizarre behavior that people have exhibited since 2020.

If you pay people to lie, most people will lie. It's sad but true, and many have enriched themselves through the Covid deception. The government created tremendous incentives for hospitals to diagnose patients with Covid, regardless of their condition. If a hospital diagnosed a patient with pneumonia, it received about $4,500 from Medicare. For Covid, it received about $13,000, and if a Covid patient ended up on a ventilator, the hospital received a generous $39,000. That's a nice chunk of change, and it explains why hospitals have joyfully participated in the scam. Hospitals of course applied pressure on their doctors to go along, and most doctors went along to keep their jobs. But some doctors didn't go along, and many of them have been quite vocal. In July 2020, an organization of doctors was formed to expose the scam, and let people know about very safe and effective ways to treat Covid. They are called *America's Frontline Doctors*, and they started out with about 2,000 members. Their first press conference took place in front of the Supreme Court in July, 2020. It should come as no surprise that the media immediately launched a vicious attack against them. Despite the fact that these doctors represent hundreds of thousands like-minded physicians around the world, and despite the fact that their treatments have proved to be amazingly effective, the professional liars were able to convince much of the public that they are quacks. What most people don't seem to realize is that when you add up all the health "experts" who've been in the spotlight and who've been running the scam, *they number less than 100!* The only thing that has given this handful of liars and quacks any credibility at all is the talking box.

Did the liars and quacks tell us anything at all that was true during the Covid hysteria they created? For example, was there any legitimate justification for locking down the country? Sweden, South Korea, Taiwan, Singapore, and Japan did not lock down their countries, and they apparently managed quite well. The reported Covid fatalities in these countries have been on par or lower than in most of the ones with lockdowns. Much, much lower than in ours. Please consider the following studies, which show the ineffectiveness of lockdowns: A study published in *The Lancet* medical journal concluded with the words, *"government actions such as border closures, full lockdowns, and a high rate of COVID-19 testing were not associated with statistically significant reductions in the number of critical cases or overall mortality."* Several months later, a study was published by *Frontiers in Public Health,* which examined data from 160 countries over a period of eight months, and which concluded with the words, *"stringency of the measures settled to fight pandemia, including lockdown, did not appear to be linked with death rate."* A Tel Aviv University study concluded with the following: *"We would have expected to see fewer Covid-19 fatalities in countries with a tighter lockdown, but the data reveals that this is not the case."* And finally, a study by Icahn School of Medicine at Mount Sinai and published in the *New England Journal of Medicine* has found that strict quarantine, tightly controlled social distancing, and the continuous use of masks, did absolutely nothing to contain the spread of Covid-19 and might even have increased its spread! It appears that many Americans have been deceived by some very convincing liars.

Globalists and their agents love to make predictions about the future, and as we've seen, they're never wrong. They made the unlikely prediction that Covid would be here for 18 months or more. They got that one right. They predicted a second wave of Covid for the fall of 2020, an October surprise. They got that one right as well. In the middle of the summer of 2020, they repeatedly predicted election chaos in November. Once again, they absolutely nailed it. I'm sure that by now, everyone can understand why they're never wrong about their predictions. Over the years, they have staged some spectacular productions, and most people would be shocked if they knew how many major events of the modern era have been staged by them. Those wishing to see a few of their productions and the unimaginable wealth of just one globalist family, may wish to read a superbly documented book entitled *Killing The Planet: How A Financial Cartel Doomed Mankind.*

One of the things they've been staging for years is the chaos we saw after the death of George Floyd. They've used their media outlets for as long as I can remember to stoke racial hatred and to disseminate the idea that America is a deeply racist country. This of course is utterly ridiculous. For the last few decades, America has been one of the *least* racist countries on earth. When we look back at our history, that's an extraordinary achievement, and it's one of the things that Americans can genuinely feel good about. However, like every other nation, America has some stains in its past, and the globalists couldn't resist exploiting one of those stains for their nefarious purposes. The race hustlers and agitators, who work ceaselessly to divide friends, neighbors, families, and entire communities, have been the most welcome guests on their media outlets for years. By giving these con artists a platform, and by branding them courageous social justice warriors, the media gradually prepared America for the riots of 2020. The globalists seized upon an issue that hasn't been a problem in America for more than fifty years, and diabolically turned it into a huge one. In fact, they've turned it into a problem so huge that it may well destroy our nation.

In my opinion, the death of George Floyd looked staged, but staged or not, what followed is all the evidence we need that the *riots* were staged. The entire cascade of riots would never have happened, had the first one in Minneapolis been stopped. But those that had the power to stop it, decided that it would be much better if the mayhem spread across the nation. We witnessed something in the summer of 2020 that I don't believe any society in world history has *ever* witnessed. The forces of law and order *standing down*, as the forces of anarchy and destruction were taking over the streets.

Many mayors and governors felt that the best way to prove to the world that they weren't racists, was to allow their cities to burn and be destroyed. Many in the media applauded the destruction to prove that *they* weren't racists, and some people made their stand against racism by apologizing for the color of their skin. Many Americans did indeed prove something to the world in the summer of 2020, but it wasn't what they intended to prove. *What they proved is that they lost their moral compass, and that they lost their minds!*

The standing down of law and order for months is the *only* evidence we need that the riots of 2020 were staged, but there's more. One example of this staging were piles of bricks that mysteriously appeared at the riot sites. The rioters were not only encouraged by many in the media and many politicians, but they were directly assisted by unknown persons with a lot of money, a lot of trucks, and a lot of bricks. The fact that the media never even mentioned this is further evidence that the chaos was staged and orchestrated.

When *Black Lives Matter* came on the scene a few years ago, many in the media embraced the movement. Perhaps they could justify this to themselves, because of a slogan that no decent person could argue against. However, every decent person can and should argue against an organization that proclaims itself to be Marxist/Communist. Should we support the Mafia if it comes up with a catchy slogan?

Unfortunately, some in the media are also Marxists/Communists, which explains their love affair with radicals and agitators. It also explains their continual harping about imaginary injustices, their magnifying relatively minor injustices into earth-shaking events, and their incitement of violence. It's an obvious fact that everyone in the world is more or less privileged than someone else. In America, some whites are more privileged than some blacks and some blacks are more privileged than some whites. The term *"white privilege"* therefore is utterly meaningless. Particularly in *this* nation, at *this* time. The truth of the matter is that the vast majority of Americans, regardless of their ethnic background or skin shade are hugely more privileged than most of the people in the rest of the world, and most of the people who've ever lived. The problem isn't systemic injustice, systemic racism, or a lack of privilege, but rather a lack of gratitude to the Lord for all the privileges we *do* have.

There does exist a certain kind of privilege however, which *is* at the root of most societal problems. The privilege I'm talking about is *super rich privilege,* and I challenge all the social justice warriors in the media to harp about this particular injustice. Most of the world's wealth is concentrated in the hands of a few thousand of the super rich. These people own or control practically all media outlets in America, and they use these outlets to divide Americans along a thousand fronts. The more divided we become as a nation, the more money and power they accumulate. The faces we see on TV belong to people who are filthy rich themselves, and most of them don't serve the interests of the people, but the interests of their corporate bosses. Please remember this fact the next time some friendly TV news anchor or some celebrity tries to persuade you about some issue. Whatever agenda or cause they're pushing, be aware that they're getting paid huge sums of money to do so, and that it's almost never for our good.

Just as promised, we saw election chaos. Everything about it was as fake as the "pandemic" and the riots. For months, we were told that masks can prevent the transmission of a virus, yet we were discouraged from going to the polls and encouraged to mail in our ballots. Right on cue, we heard story after story about mail carriers who dumped bags of mail into garbage dumpsters. Interestingly, these mail carriers seemed to prefer dumping the mail at locations that had surveillance cameras, so the nation could see it. Stories such as these prepared the public to question the integrity of the 2020 election, and at the same time to unquestioningly accept the election chaos as just another random event.

During a busy election, results can be a few hours late, but they can't be days late. If the count takes days, the recount can't take weeks. Inasmuch as the globalists own or control all the major news networks, there shouldn't be any significant *factual* discrepancies between their various networks. Fox presented their viewers with evidence of election fraud, while CNN maintains to this day that no such evidence exists. If both are owned or controlled by the same people, this doesn't make sense. It makes perfect sense however, when you understand the real reason that this occurs so frequently. Those who only view Fox can't understand why their neighbors who only view CNN can be so stupid. CNN viewers feel the same way about their Fox viewing neighbors. It's a very simple strategy to polarize the country and create chaos.

By design, the two networks are on opposite ends of our nation's culture war. One of them does tell the public much more truth than the other, while its counterpart spreads misinformation and twists facts 24/7 about every issue. However, people should notice the one thing they both have in common. *Neither network has ever exposed the crimes of the globalists.* Both networks have deceived the public about 9/11, and while Fox may have pointed out some of the absurdities related to the Covid crisis, it never informed the public that it was a staged event. Inasmuch as the network played an essential role in staging it, how could it? Whether we buy Coke or Pepsi, the money we spend is enriching the very same people. In a similar fashion, whether we watch CNN or Fox, the power structure of the globalists remains intact, and they remain free to commit more crimes. They hide themselves in plain sight behind their very own corporations, whether those corporations lean to the left or the right. They hide themselves in exactly the same way behind the two major political parties. While Democrats and Republicans may put on a great public show of fighting each other, very few of them expose the criminals at the top who are essentially running everything. They can't of course, because whichever party they belong to, most of them were put into office with the backing of the globalists.

2020 has indeed been a year of staged events and psychological operations. It started with a relatively mild, seasonal flu type virus, which was presented to the public as the return of the "Black Death." It continued with lockdowns, mask mandates, curfews, and countless other nonsensical restrictions. We witnessed the destruction of our economy, as hundreds of thousands of small businesses were forced into bankruptcy. Millions of Americans lost their homes to the banks or were evicted, and our national debt has skyrocketed. But all of this still wasn't enough for the globalists and their agents. They decided that the nation needed riots and massive civil unrest, so we watched our cities burn. But even that wasn't enough for them, so they prepared election chaos for our nation, the consequences of which are still felt today. There have been other staged events and psychological operations since 2020, and those who think critically should be able to identify them quite easily. The idea behind much that has happened the last few years was to tear down the social fabric, and to create so much chaos and confusion, that a significant segment of our population can barely think at all.

Throughout most of our nation's history, a clandestine criminal gang has been steering the country in a certain direction from behind the scenes. They've been staging wars, causing market crashes, and creating all kinds of mayhem that has hugely enriched them. In 2020, they pulled out all the stops and unleashed total destruction on the country we love. Their objective is to bring America to its knees. Despite the fact that they have made their presence known in numerous ways in the past, and that they are operating quite openly today, most Americans still refuse to acknowledge that this criminal gang even exists.

TRAITORS, TYRANTS, AGENTS, SHILLS, AND SHEEPLE

In this chapter, we'll take a brief look at the leading actors in the Covid drama. They can be divided into two major categories. The deceivers and the deceived. It shouldn't be too difficult to figure out which category the sheeple fit in. A third category has been steadily growing. Those who are waking up.

When deceivers deceive, only a tiny percentage do it just for fun. Most of them do it for money and power, and since 2020, a lot of very wicked people have accumulated an awful lot of money and power. The sheeple lost both as usual, but they don't seem to mind all that much. They're just thankful someone cared enough to keep them safe.

First, let us define our terms. According to the dictionary, traitors are those who betray their country, a trust, or a cause. When someone gives their allegiance to a foreign power and takes directives from that power to subvert their own country, we call such a person a traitor. It can be argued that the globalist cabal, consisting of many individuals who are not even American citizens, is a foreign power. But that's a legal matter, and I'll let the lawyers sort it out. When I use the word "traitor," I use it in the sense of someone betraying a trust or a cause. An example of this would be a governor who has taken an oath to uphold and defend the Constitution of the United States, and who has violated it. The word "tyrant" doesn't need much explanation. It's someone who issues orders and threats, and who has the power to make good on those threats. An "agent" is a representative of an organization such as a government, but agents often work undercover, so they could be anyone. And finally, a "shill" is someone who pretends to be a disinterested observer, but is really part of the con game. A perfect example of a shill would be a TV doctor who gets paid for promoting drugs and vaccines. The traitors, tyrants, agents, and shills connected to Covid came mostly from the media, the medical establishment, and the government.

The globalist cabal handled the business aspect of the great Covid deception. To maximize the deception and capture everyone in its orbit, their businesses predictably took the lead in instituting all manner of safety procedures to keep their employees and customers safe. Fast food restaurant chains closed their dining areas, and only served customers via a drive-thru. They immediately mandated masks for their employees and customers, and they spent inordinate amounts of money on signs and plastic barriers. These plastic barriers, which serve absolutely no purpose as far as viruses are concerned, have become a permanent fixture in some of their businesses. The only purpose they serve is as a continual visual reminder to the gullible that something very, very dangerous is on the other side. Some businesses closed certain entrances during the height of Covid hysteria, to show the public how seriously they were taking the pandemic. The logic behind this was a little weak, inasmuch as crowding people into fewer entrances defeated the purpose of social distancing, but it did create a better show. To make the show even more believable, they designated certain employees to sanitize shopping carts and conveyor belts. The actors in all their commercials wore masks, and it made a person wonder whether they were selling products and services or masks. They also made sure not to leave the children out, as evidenced by one commercial in which a little girl was playing with dolls, all wearing masks. If there's one thing the globalists understand better than anything else, it's how to recruit the next generation when they're young. Get Johnny and Susie on board, and they'll remind Mom and Dad not to forget their masks. Santa Claus was of course wearing a mask. He told all the children to wear one too, and to not forget to get their shots. To conjure up images in our minds of a nuclear apocalypse, we were treated to repeated video clips of hospital personnel dressed up in hazmat suits. If one paid close attention however, one could see that many of those clips were stock footage repeated over and over. It's all been quite a theatrical production, and everyone was forced to be part of the cast. Enlisting widespread public participation was essential for transforming the country into a giant lunatic asylum.

One of the most popular and amusing shows on TV was New York Governor Cuomo's daily Covid briefing. When the lunacy started, he entered the spotlight and decided to never leave it. He selflessly gave his time to help the nation fight the horrible scourge of Covid. Governor Cuomo informed us about overcrowded hospitals, logistical problems, a shortage of ventilators, quarantines, social distancing, and the proper wearing of masks. He shared anecdotes, friendly words of wisdom, and administered stern rebukes to those not taking the crisis seriously. The governor told us way more about Covid than we wanted to know, and if he was still in office, he might be telling us more. Perhaps his funniest line came while giving a stern rebuke to young people for going outside. He told the offenders that they shouldn't be killing his grandma. You can't make this stuff up. To this day, I haven't yet figured out whether Governor Cuomo's briefings were designed for 4 or 5 year olds.

The show became such a huge hit that other governors got in on the action. There's nothing like a little free airtime, and being a governor is after all just a step from being president. The governors knew very well what the globalists were up to, and they also knew that when their one-world government eventually comes into being, prominent positions in that government will be offered to the most decisive and charismatic leaders. So, they were essentially auditioning for those positions. The governors were also aware of the fact that the more brutally they treated their constituents, the better the globalists would like it. I commend the few governors, mayors, and other public officials who did not participate in the great Covid deception, and who treated their fellow citizens with some measure of decency.

The ridiculous edicts, the draconian restrictions, and the flagrant Constitutional violations by public officials are a national disgrace that will long be remembered. But because the tyrants were so numerous, few people at the time questioned their criminal actions. Instead of being a check on government tyranny, most in the media applauded the tyranny and empowered it. There were only a handful of bright lights in the entire mainstream media cesspool during the height of Covid hysteria. Tucker Carlson and Laura Ingraham on Fox were two of those bright lights, and they deserve a special mention. They weren't allowed to say everything that could have been said, but I get the sense that they said as much as they could.

A major source of alternative information in the past has been the internet. It's never been the gold standard for truth, because agents, shills, disinformation channels, globalist fronts, and run of the mill liars have dominated it from its inception. But it *was* possible to find some truth there if one dug long and hard. All that changed dramatically in 2020. Social media and YouTube began censoring content that in any way questioned the official Covid narrative. Iranian Ayatollahs were allowed to say anything they wanted, but not American doctors who disagreed with Dr. Fauci. One after another, videos were removed, and accounts were cancelled. The standard justification was *"spreading medical misinformation."* I find this very puzzling, because inasmuch as those doing the cancelling were not licensed medical professionals, how could they possibly know what is and what isn't medical misinformation? But even if these self-appointed censors *were* licensed medical professionals, would that in any way make their opinions more valid than the opinions of other licensed medical professionals? Massive censorship on the internet began with Covid, but later it was expanded to *any* information the owners of the internet platforms wished to suppress. The election of Donald Trump has changed things significantly, because the globalists are ever mindful of massive pushback by the public. It is important however, to remember that while their strategy may have changed, their agenda has not. It has simply been delayed.

Who gave the great Covid deception credibility and who kept it going? I'd say it's a handful of health "experts" from the World

Health Organization, another handful from the CDC, Dr. Fauci, and a couple dozen TV doctors. It's difficult to believe, but all it has taken to work this scam is a few key people, in a few key positions! When it comes to Covid, the voices of hundreds of thousands of doctors around the world didn't count, but the voices of a handful of con artists did.

There are various fields of science and they're based upon logic, reason, the laws of physics, and principles that people can generally understand. But there is an entirely new branch of science that was developed in 2020, which only truly gifted "experts" can understand. A good name for it would be Covid Science. It's an extremely complicated branch of science that has baffled many people, but we can be thankful that we have Covid scientists who can make sense of it. Here are a few examples of how Covid Science works and how it is saving humanity:

Many people have questioned the logic of curfews, but according to Covid scientists, the virus, much like the boogeyman, is nocturnal. Only a fool would argue with science.

Covid scientists are all in agreement that wearing a mask provides perfect protection against the virus – but *only* if everyone is wearing one too. That's Covid Science 101.

It has been suggested by Covid Science experts that people not only quarantine at home, but that they also cut off all outside airflow, using plastic and duct tape. This may cause problems if you walk your dog three times a day or need oxygen to breathe, but Covid Science recommends potty training your dog and getting an oxygen tank.

Stores in some places allowed the purchase of only certain items. Covid Science experts felt such measures were absolutely necessary for slowing the spread of the virus.

When a baby refused to wear a mask on an airplane, the baby and its parents were quickly escorted off the plane. Fellow passengers were mercifully saved from a health disaster, due to the quick thinking of airline officials and the latest advances in Covid Science.

A man took his mask off to get a drink from a water fountain. A nearby police officer fined him $100 for not wearing a mask. A woman received a $100 fine, because her mask didn't cover her nose. More lives saved thanks to Covid Science.

You were allowed to take your mask off if you were eating or drinking at a restaurant, but you absolutely had to wear it when going to the restroom, because that's when the virus attacks. That's basic Covid Science.

You were not allowed to try on a garment at the store, because you might have infected it. You could however, infect it at home and return it an hour later. To some people this didn't make sense, but it makes perfect Covid Science sense.

Many governors determined that businesses such as liquor stores and abortion clinics were essential services. They also determined that gyms and churches were not. These decisions were based on the latest Covid Science research.

Wearing a mask at home, in your car, or when the nearest person was miles away was highly recommended, because according to leading Covid scientists, virus particles fly around the planet like migratory birds and they could land anywhere.

Some people have been brutally beaten by the police in some parts of the world for not wearing a mask. Strict adherence to Covid Science guidelines inspired such heroic actions, and there's no telling how many lives were saved.

The world owes a debt of gratitude to all the Covid scientists at the WHO, the CDC, as well as to our very own Dr. Fauci. Their brilliance is unequaled and their tireless efforts on behalf of humanity have been truly inspiring!

We may perhaps get a chuckle out of this, but none of it is funny to people who lost the roof over their heads, or who had their lives utterly destroyed by this scam. But the tyrants aren't finished yet, because every small business in America isn't bankrupt yet. There's also a small measure of freedom left, and that can't be allowed to stand. Some of our elected representatives who work for the globalists, while pretending to work for the American people, have gone too far to turn back. The best they can hope for now is that they get to their New World Order, or their Great Reset, or to whatever sick police state they've dreamed up, before the American people wake up and they have to answer for their crimes.

You can have all the traitors, tyrants, agents, and shills you want, but the train isn't leaving the station without the most essential players, the sheeple. Once they're on board, you can travel to just about any destination. Hitler and all his thugs could have accomplished nothing without the acquiescence of millions of ordinary Germans. He didn't need them to become ardent fans of his, or to participate in any of his atrocities. All he needed them to do was shut their mouths, close their eyes, and blindly go along. What Hitler absolutely had to have is a nation full of sheeple. This is what every psychopath has to have if he wishes to wreak havoc upon a society.

The basic difference between people and sheeple is this: People thoughtfully consider what they're being told, ask questions, and take appropriate action. In contrast, sheeple always accept what they're told without question, and always follow and obey. The nightmare of 2020 has made it clear that America has more sheeple than even the globalists could have wished for. Some of them are now waking up and are becoming people again, but the cost of so many being sheeple for so long is astronomical. It's astronomical for millions of Americans whose lives have been destroyed, and it's astronomical for the nation as a whole.

The American people didn't suddenly become sheeple in 2020. The majority have been sheeple for generations. Most don't have a clue what the Revolutionary War was all about, or what freedom even means. They would have a difficult time believing that in many ways, the British government of King George was *less* tyrannical than the government we have now. Perhaps this is because history and political science textbooks are inaccurate, incomplete, and misleading, which is a polite way of saying that much of what they contain is a pack of lies.

Sheeple desire two things above all else. They want someone to tell them fairy tales and someone to keep them safe. Luckily for them, Big Brother is always ready and willing to fulfill these desires. We've all read about Big Brother in school, how while pretending to be gentle and caring, he was really just a big, bad, psychopathic wolf. It's amazing to see that many Americans who got the message that the fictional Big Brother wasn't nice at all, also believe wholeheartedly that the real one is. What then was the point of reading the book?

People in general and sheeple in particular want to be lied to, so we shouldn't be surprised that many of our leaders and many so-called journalists have very generously accommodated us. There would have been no Covid deception, had the public awakened to the truth of 9/11. The Lord gave us nineteen years to do so, but most Americans would rather undergo a root canal than read a book or watch a documentary about 9/11. As a result, God gave our nation what it so dearly desired. Nineteen years of lies, culminating with the big one of 2020. For those unfamiliar with the Bible, please allow me to inform you that one of God's most common ways of judging people or nations, is to give them exactly what they want.

Because of Covid, as well as a host of other deceptions inundating our nation, America has become a giant lunatic asylum, and there's only one way out. We got in through lies, so the way out is through truth. In reality, those running the asylum are the crazy ones, so anyone who wants out, needs to put those running it *in*. A good place to start would be with most of the talking heads on TV. They need to be laughed right off the air, and if they happen to be politicians, they need to be laughed right out of office. They may be crazy like foxes, because they're pursuing some kind of self-serving agenda, but most people would agree that destroying one's own nation for *any* reason is insane!

MASKS

Perhaps the most distinguishing feature of our society since 2020 have been masks. They've become so popular, some Americans never want to take them off. We've seen masks at the workplace and outside the workplace. Masks at grocery stores and at every other place of business. Masks at churches and in dens of iniquity. Masks indoors and outdoors. Masks at schools, and perhaps most importantly, masks on television. We have even seen masks at riots. Everywhere we've looked, we've seen masks, masks, and more masks!

So, what's the real story behind the mask madness we have witnessed? We might say it's related to the shortcomings of previous scams the globalists have worked upon the public. For example, the war on terror was a great scam, but its major shortcoming was the fact that it wasn't interactive. A few months after 9/11, most people didn't give a hoot about terrorists, or about what was happening on the other side of the world. The globalists needed a scam that involved continued public participation. Coming up with a pandemic was brilliant, but inserting masks into it was an absolute stroke of genius.

Out of the less than 100 health "experts" who've been running the Covid operation, not a single one of them has ever cited a single study that shows the efficacy of wearing masks to slow the transmission of a virus. The reason for this is simple. *No such study exists.* All the studies done show the exact opposite. So, why have so many followed their recommendations in regard to masks? The reason for that is simple as well. *Because they're experts, because they're on TV, and because they said so.* But don't doctors and nurses sometimes wear masks? Yes, when in very close proximity to very vulnerable patients or during surgeries, doctors and nurses do wear masks. They do so however, because people sometimes *cough and sneeze,* not because they *breathe.*

The reason masks are ineffective in slowing the transmission of viruses is because of the size of virus particles. The size of a virus particle is approximately .1 microns. Masks, while appearing solid, are in reality not solid at all. The size of the pores in the masks worn by the public is anywhere from 20 to 200 microns. If you do the math, this means the pores in those masks are 200 to 2,000 times larger than a virus particle. The chance of a mask keeping out virus particles is about the same as the bars of a jail cell keeping out mosquitoes. The use of face shields as protection against virus particles is even more ridiculous. The best they can do is to keep your face from getting smashed by a snowball.

That masks cannot block virus particles is common knowledge to all the health "experts" who are recommending them. It's been common knowledge for decades. Those who are skeptical however, might think *some hack writing a book can say anything, but I'd rather trust the wisdom of Dr. Fauci.* Okay then, let's put our trust in the wisdom of Dr. Fauci. In an e-mail that was obtained through a Freedom of Information Act lawsuit, this is how Dr. Fauci answered an acquaintance who inquired about this very topic:

"The typical mask you buy in the drug store is not really effective in keeping out virus, which is small enough to pass through the material." The fact that this private comment is a direct contradiction of Dr. Fauci's public pronouncements should not surprise anyone. Those running the Covid operation have been contradicting themselves and each other on an almost daily basis since the very beginning. This of course is precisely what we would expect if they were making up the Covid narrative as they went along.

To say that the globalists don't hold anyone outside their clique in very high regard would be a huge understatement. The fact is, they have utter contempt for humanity and view us as no better than cattle. This is clear from the cavalier way they discuss humanity in their *Lock Step* scenario, in *Event 201*, and in countless human guinea pig experiments they're either proposing or running.

The mask agenda is the boldest, most far-reaching mind control and social engineering experiment the globalists have ever designed for us. The experiment is obviously about instilling irrational fear and training us to respond like Pavlov's dogs, but on a deeper level, it's about changing our perception of ourselves and others. The Lord told us in the book of Genesis that we are made in His image, and this has certain implications for how we are to *see* each other and relate to each other. The mask agenda is a major step in erasing those implications.

Since masks came on the scene, we've been able to catch small glimpses of the kind of world the globalists are preparing for us, and of the kind of people they wish to turn all of us into. We've already seen what can happen when ordinary people turn into sheeple who believe and obey every tyrant who comes along. In regard to masks, the passion and fanaticism of some of them has been downright frightening. They saw themselves as brave Covid warriors, on a mission to save humanity from the greatest plague the world has ever seen. They've been told by some very sick and deranged people that a mask is part of a military uniform, and that those not wearing one are the enemy. They've also been told that those not wearing a mask are bio-terrorists. The most brainwashed sheeple never questioned these insane pronouncements, and all across the country, we saw confrontations between people and sheeple over the wearing of masks. One elderly lady was harassed by a nasty group of Covid warriors and felt so threatened, she finally yelled at them *"get away from me, you Nazis!"* That stopped them in their tracks, and they backed off. Another lady walked into a grocery store not wearing a mask, but with a printed copy of a local ordinance, which stated that no place of business can deny entrance to anyone for not wearing a mask. The store management did not challenge her, but the masked Covid warriors did. They all screamed at her, called her names, and slammed their carts into hers. She told them to read the ordinance, but they completely ignored her and continued with their enraged frenzy. It never even dawned on them that if what the "experts" told them was true, their own masks were ample protection against a virus, regardless of whether this lady was wearing one or not. But logic plays no part in brainwashing. In typical fashion, the media sided with the brainwashed lunatics, because normalizing lunacy is what the media does best. In another incident, two men were eating lunch at an outside restaurant when approached by a belligerent woman who ordered them to put on masks. When they didn't comply, she gave them the middle finger, and threw hot coffee into the face of one.

Because of massive mind control, there were countless incidents across the country, in which otherwise ordinary Americans have turned into deranged and dangerous thugs.

Meanwhile, the globalists running the scam have been laughing their heads off. They've managed to turn a significant percentage of our population into utter lunatics and to divide the American people along one more front. Their smashing success with masks has only emboldened them to deceive the public in other ways. These people didn't get to be the richest in the world because they're stupid.

When the mask mandates were first introduced, *real* doctors began warning the public about the dangers of the prolonged use of masks. The constriction of air flow leads to oxygen deprivation, which in turn suppresses the immune system. They said that in time, this would cause a medical catastrophe, which would overwhelm the health care system. But the agents, shills, and quacks got busy, and began telling the sheeple not to worry, that wearing a mask all day long for months on end is perfectly safe. Their message to the gullible was that all the talk about the constriction of air flow and oxygen deprivation is simply medical misinformation. The sheeple knew full well that a mask *does* constrict air flow, because they couldn't wait to take it off and get a full breath of fresh air. When they finally did, their own lungs told them that the air without the mask was a whole lot different than the air they'd been breathing for the last eight hours. The liars of course had an answer for this as well. They told the sheeple that what they knew to be true was just their imagination. This is when it became truly bizarre, because many sheeple actually believed these lying quacks, rather than what their own lungs were telling them! When brainwashing reaches this point, you can get the willing victims to do just about anything, and that can be catastrophic for a society that has too many of them.

Most of us know that human beings breathe in oxygen and breathe out carbon dioxide. A good number of us are also aware of the fact that carbon dioxide is a poison gas. When the Covid scientists and health "experts" told the sheeple that they're *not* breathing in their own poison gas, the sheeple naturally believed them. Many are convinced to this day that Dr. Fauci and his friends have never steered them wrong. Regarding this issue, if a mask constricts the intake of oxygen, then logic tells us it also traps some carbon dioxide. The person is then breathing back some of that carbon dioxide. Oxygen deprivation and carbon dioxide poisoning will in the long-term lead to a suppression of the immune system, which then makes a person susceptible to every kind of sickness and disease.

For anyone who has doubts about whether a mask constricts the intake of oxygen and traps carbon dioxide, I suggest a simple experiment. Put on your mask, light a candle, and then try to blow the candle out. Some may be able to do it, but when I tried it, I couldn't even come close to blowing out the candle. This should once and for all settle the issue of who the legitimate doctors and who the quacks are.

Even though the quacks, agents, and shills had been exposed for the liars they are, they were brazen enough at one point to ramp up their mask disinformation campaign to an even higher level. They began telling the public to wear N95 masks. This of course is much more dangerous to people's health, because oxygen deprivation with N95 masks is greater than with ordinary masks.

The pores in them are much smaller, but still much larger than a virus particle, which makes them just as useless.

There's no doubt that some people have done serious harm to their health by putting their faith in proven liars. In such instances, there's a shared culpability for all negative consequences. But it's different with children, because they can't make their own decisions. The psychological, emotional, and physical harm that has been inflicted on children by forcing them to wear masks for months is nothing short of criminal. That the American public has allowed this abuse for so long is an indication that mass psychosis has a tight grip on our society.

The mask propaganda we've all been subjected to since 2020 has been tiresome, and for those who are informed, it has been nauseating. For months and months, when channel surfing or watching news, not a minute went by without seeing masks. They seemed to be the most essential prop in any TV production. Sometimes the actors would slip up when they mistakenly thought the cameras weren't rolling, and the masks came off. This happened with reporters at White House news conferences, as well as with world leaders at summits. When given the signal, they all put their masks on or took them off, not realizing that a solitary camera was recording their play-acting. During the height of the mask madness, the biggest mask pushers were continually being caught on camera without a mask. This happened so much that it became a standing joke, and it should have awakened everyone to the fact that we were in the middle of a show.

The inconsistencies and absurdities related to the Covid show are so numerous that they could almost wake the dead. So, why are so many sheeple still sleeping? One reason may be that there are so many of them, which gives them assurance that they are right. There is a herd instinct in all of us, and everyone knows that a herd can't be wrong. Except of course when they're going over a cliff, like happened in Nazi Germany in the 1930's, and hundreds of other times in human history. But many believe that such a thing can't possibly happen to us, because we are much, much smarter than all those stupid people that came before us. The simple truth is that once you get enough people behind a particular media-driven cause, then that cause begins to pick up steam and avalanche, even if it's utter madness. Eventually, even the skeptics join the cause, because of the mind-numbing 24/7 propaganda. In such circumstances, it generally doesn't take very long before an entire nation begins to go over a cliff.

Please allow me to illustrate how easy it was to brainwash an entire nation about masks. In addition to what the professional liars had to say about the issue, Public Service Announcements were being run hour after hour on practically all radio and television stations all across the country. The basic message of these PSA's was to extoll the virtues of masks and to shame those who don't wear them. If one truly cares about their loved ones, their friends and neighbors, then the only possible thing to do is to wear a mask. Only selfish, non-caring, and hateful people refuse to wear a mask. The most fanatical sheeple joined their voices to the propaganda blitz, and all voices of sanity were eventually drowned out. Here's an example of the type of video that appeared on social media by the hundreds: A man gave a list of medical conditions which might prevent someone from wearing a mask. They are: *"Science-Itis," "Acute Wussness," "Selfish Syndrome," "Chronic Dickishness," "Pathological Ignorance,"* and *"Severe Moron-ness."* He closed the video with the following words: *"If you suffer from one of those conditions and don't want to wear a mask, just stay home. Seriously, don't go out, and stay the hell away from me, and let the rest of us just get on with it."* Here's a question for all my readers: Do you think it would be possible to have a reasoned, logical discussion with this man about masks? Personally, I wouldn't attempt to have one, because he's either a government disinformation agent who knows that what he's saying is lunacy, or he's brainwashed beyond help. The most frightening thing isn't a handful of lunatics or government agents spouting off on social media. The most frightening thing is the fact that millions of Americans believe this lunacy.

One side of the propaganda coin has been to shame and ridicule those who are informed about the uselessness and dangers of masks. The other side of that coin has been to present masks to the public as the best thing since sliced bread. Here's a portion of one TV commercial that did just that: *"This is not a mask, this is confidence. This is not a mask, this is solidarity. This is not a mask, this is a sign of love."* How does a person respond to something like this? I've thought long and hard about these bizarre words and tried to categorize them. The best that I could come up with is *deranged gibberish*. The fact of the matter is that this is just one example in an avalanche of deranged gibberish we have been subjected to in our nation for years. We live in a time when very few people seem to be concerned about the consequences of anything, but I would suggest that when deranged gibberish becomes the norm in a nation, that nation is in the final stage of its demise.

Our nation's economy has been ruined for many years to come as a result of the Covid show, but there's one sector of the economy that thrived during the show. Anything to do with masks, around which a cottage industry quickly arose. They became a fashion statement, and there was a demand for custom masks. It was a great way to tell people about ourselves. Instead of talking, we could just put on masks. Whatever we wished to communicate to the world could be communicated with masks. For example, patriots could wear a mask with an American flag, and Communists could wear one with a hammer and sickle. Smiley faces became popular, and the great thing about them was that when we were feeling sad, we could wear them upside down. Wearing a mask made it possible for us to tell the world virtually anything, so you might say that this bizarre fad has been a welcome innovation for shy people. In my opinion, the custom mask with the most appropriate message is the one that says SHEEPLE.

Die-hard believers in the effectiveness of masks may wish to read the label the next time they buy a box. All state clearly that the masks are for non-medical use only, but some clarify this by specifically stating things such as: *This mask is not designed to protect you from Covid-19 or from any other virus.* If that's the case, why did anyone ever wear one? More importantly, if masks can't protect you, and if they can even cause serious health problems, then why were people forced to wear them? I think you already know the answer to that question, but I'll add one final comment. Masks have historically been a symbol of silencing, submission, and slavery. One of the ways slave owners would punish and humiliate their human property was to muzzle them with a mask. In addition to being master psychologists, the globalists are also excellent students of history.

In 2020, most people put on masks. In the same year, others took their masks off, and we got a good look at their little, black hearts. The media deceivers would label me an "anti-masker," because derogatory labels are always an absolute must for anyone who doesn't buy into their lies. But they've got it all wrong. I'm not anti-mask or an "anti-masker," because I firmly believe there are appropriate times to wear a mask. *I am however, anti-ignorance, and I am most definitely anti-brainwashing!*

VACCINES

Sometimes, the best way to get to the truth of a matter is to simply ask a few questions. In this chapter, I'll ask a couple questions, and perhaps we can clear up some confusion about the subject of vaccines.

Imagine that you were elected to Congress, and when you got to Washington, one of your constituents sent you $100 for your re-election campaign. Imagine again that another party sent you $100,000. Finally, let's imagine that sometime during your term, a vote came up about an issue over which both of your supporters disagreed. How would you vote on that particular issue? The way the $100 supporter wanted, or the way the $100,000 supporter wanted? If you went with the big bucks, then you now have a pretty good idea of how Washington has worked from the beginning. *It's the way every government has always worked.*

Here's another theoretical scenario. Let's suppose you were a doctor, and one of the TV networks offered you a multi-million dollar contract to be one of their in-house medical experts. Let's suppose further that you were given a fairly free reign to say whatever you wanted, but with one stipulation. You could never say anything negative about vaccines or pharmaceutical companies.

Would you agree to the contract? If you answered yes, then you know the most important thing to know about TV doctors.

If a certain car model developed problems, and it led to the injury or death of a substantial number of people, that model would then be immediately recalled by the manufacturer. If a certain cell phone or TV model began to explode, and it led to the injury or death of a substantial number of people, those models would also be immediately recalled by the manufacturers. In both cases, the companies would have a financial liability for the damage they caused, and people would have a legal recourse to be compensated by those companies. What legal recourse do people have when a pharmaceutical company injures or kills someone with one of their vaccines? *Absolutely none!*

Most people who hear this think, *that can't be, this is America, where anyone can sue anyone over anything.* Yes, anyone and anything, *except a pharmaceutical company for a vaccine injury!* It is a little-known fact that in 1986, Congress passed one of the greatest legislative abominations in the history of the country, exempting vaccine manufacturers from any liability due to damage caused by their vaccines. It is called *The National Childhood Vaccine Injury Act.* Our elected representatives felt this law was needed, because a flood of lawsuits against pharmaceutical companies were making their way to the courts as a result of horrendous vaccine injuries. These lawsuits had the potential to bankrupt the entire pharmaceutical industry. The law Congress passed set up a special "Vaccine Injury Court," that is unlike any regular court. First of all, there is no jury, and the burden of proof for an injury is almost impossible to meet. Secondly, the maximum amount that can be awarded is only $250,000, which is a pittance for parents who must take care of a crippled child for the rest of their lives. And thirdly, not a penny of that money comes from the pharmaceutical companies, but from the National Treasury. It's not those who caused the damage that pay, it's the taxpayers. The entire setup is nothing but a charade, and a mockery of families whose lives have been turned into a living nightmare. Today, there are multitudes of such families around the world. This 1986 law is a testimony to the callousness of many of our elected representatives, as well as clear evidence of whose interests they serve.

Despite this, you will see an endless number of agents, shills, and quacks on TV, who tell you with a straight face that vaccines have always been perfectly safe. It's easy to understand why so many people would be motivated to tell such an outrageous and easily refutable lie, when we consider the mind-boggling profits of pharmaceutical companies. We're not talking millions or billions, but in the long run, *trillions!* The Covid vaccine alone could net them more than a trillion. If they should succeed in creating a precedent for mandatory global vaccination, because of Covid or some other disease, they may eventually be able to mandate the entire spectrum of vaccines to the entire population of the planet. If that should happen, the profits of the pharmaceutical companies would be unimaginable.

Detectives know that when you follow the money, you can unravel a lot of mysteries, and the Word of God tells us that *"the love of money is the root of all evil."* Keeping this in mind, much of what happened in 2020 begins to make perfect sense. When the virus played out in China in March with less than 5,000 fatalities, and when there were around 100 fatalities in America, we were already being told that the "pandemic" wouldn't end until there was a vaccine. Other than masks and riots, vaccines became the hottest topic of the year. In fact, when you think about it, *2020 was nothing but one giant vaccine commercial!*

The history of vaccines is a story of frauds, cover-ups, and obstruction of justice. The corruption related to the vaccine industry can only be matched by the corruption in banking. The toll in terms of human destruction is incalculable. When carefully examined, even its successes turn out to be a manipulation of existing data and statistics, as well as the omission of other relevant data. Those who are willing to look at the evidence objectively, must inevitably conclude that vaccines have done at least as much harm as good. That evidence however, is continually being suppressed. Whenever a small fire of incriminating information and truth starts to spread, the TV doctors and a multitude of other liars immediately try to stamp it out. The public thinks they look so honest, they can't possibly be lying. What the public doesn't realize however, is that when shills are being hired, honest looks are the number one qualification for the job. The TV networks are searching for people who look like the clean-cut boy next door, the young lady who looks like a virgin, or someone who looks like a kindly old grandfather. Could these people be themselves deceived when they talk about the proven safety of vaccines? I suppose anything is possible, but in order for that to have happened, they'd have to be massively uninformed, or massively stupid. I don't believe either one of those is very likely. It's much more likely that they are exactly what they appear to be, professional liars!

The shills, agents, and quacks are often quite helpful. They don't want busy people wasting their precious time on nonsense like books or documentaries about vaccines. One shill, agent or quack has a video on YouTube, in which he let's us know that he watched the documentary *VAXXED*, so we wouldn't be unduly burdened by watching it. It seems that he and others like him, have made it their life's mission to make sure that no one ever learns about the unspeakable horrors that lie at the heart of the vaccine controversy. Their message is always the same, *"you can trust us, we're doctors!"* Most of the public doesn't really care, and swallows their mumbo-jumbo, hook, line, and sinker. It takes way too much mental strain to think about things like vaccines, and besides, Wheel of Fortune is coming on! A number of years ago, I came across a very informative documentary called *Vaccine Nation,* and the most striking thing about it was how many views it had. *A pitiful 131, and I was viewer 132!* Later, I came across a very popular cartoon video entitled *Marshmallow Man vs American Ninja – Will Mello Prevail?* It had close to 40 million views! When a Taylor Swift or an Eminem video shows up, it sometimes has over 100 million views! This tells us a lot about the priorities of most people in today's society, and it also tells us that most of them prefer ignorance over knowledge. It's no wonder that the Covid deception was so easy to pull off. Someone should inform the American people that ignorance can sometimes be deadly.

The link between certain kinds of vaccines and autism has been established beyond *any* doubt, but the medical "experts" continue to deny, deny, deny! Before the 1930's, autism was unknown. By the 1970's about 1 in 10,000 children were diagnosed with autism, and the number of children affected has been steadily rising. Today, it is about 1 in 30 children, and it is estimated that by 2032, it will be 1 in 2 children! But don't worry, nothing's really going on. One TV medical "expert" had the gall to say that we don't know what's causing autism, but we know that it's definitely not vaccines. This is the type of logic you will often hear from the "experts." They don't know what it is, but they definitely know what it isn't! When I went to school, if I displayed such logic in my homework assignments, I'd get an F, and my teacher would send me for an IQ test.

Doctors, scientists, and researchers who discovered the truth about vaccines and who've spoken about it publicly, have had their reputations trashed, their careers destroyed, and have even been jailed! This is perhaps one of the best indicators of where the truth lies in regard to vaccines. It's not difficult to believe that people would lie to advance their careers and make more money, but who in their right mind would throw away everything for a lie? The shills have repeatedly been challenged to debate the issue publicly, but they have repeatedly declined. They're very smug and arrogant when pontificating in front of a camera, but it's very easy to win a debate when you're the only one holding a microphone.

On July 23, 2020, an extraordinary event took place. It was a vaccine debate between Alan Dershowitz, one of the most brilliant legal minds in the country, and Robert F. Kennedy Jr., an attorney and an outspoken advocate for people whose children have been irreparably harmed by vaccines. The debate was moderated by Patrick Bet-David. It began with Alan Dershowitz lobbing a couple of cannonballs at Robert Kennedy who swatted them away like flies. His knowledge of the subject was encyclopedic. As the debate continued, Alan Dershowitz stopped lobbing cannonballs, and resorted to a peashooter. The whole thing was embarrassing to watch, because every round Robert Kennedy was scoring more points, and his opponent had less and less to say. It became obvious very quickly that Alan Dershowitz came into the debate, armed with nothing more than the propaganda of the TV doctors. I encourage everyone to watch this debate, and to determine for yourself who won. When it was over, Patrick Bet-David issued a challenge to anyone who wanted to take on Robert Kennedy in a future debate. I don't believe anyone has yet accepted the challenge, and I strongly suspect no one ever will. After seeing this debate, I'm convinced Robert Kennedy would make mincemeat out of anyone that did.

Dr. Judy Mikovits, a former highly respected research scientist in the area of retroviruses, had her career destroyed and her reputation trashed. She was viciously attacked, because through her research she discovered a link between vaccines and certain debilitating health conditions. The link was animal viruses that sometimes made it into vaccines, because one of the ingredients in their manufacture is animal cell tissue. She was arrested without a warrant and spent five days in jail. Something we might expect in a place like China if one exposed government corruption, or veered from the official narrative. Later, she was put under a gag order, and for years she was not allowed to speak publicly. Yes, all of this happened in America, and all of it was related to her speaking publicly about the dangers of vaccines. Dr. Mikovits is the author of the best-selling book *Plague of Corruption*. She also took part in the making of the 2020 documentary *Plandemic*, an exposé of the Covid scam and vaccines. The documentary was almost immediately banned by YouTube and other platforms. In July of 2020, the Sinclair Broadcast Group that owns or operates about 300 TV stations around the country was set to air her documentary. But mysteriously, just hours before air-time, the broadcast was canceled. Having watched it, I can understand why. If it aired, there's a very good chance that the nation would have awakened to the Covid scam, and that some people would now be in prison.

There was a reason that *America's Frontline Doctors* were so viciously attacked by the media. They put a serious monkey wrench in the entire Covid operation, which may have brought it to a screeching halt in the very beginning. Representing hundreds of thousands like-minded physicians around the world, they have been treating their Covid patients with very safe and effective remedies, and have a success rate of almost 100%. But one of the main objectives of the Covid operation was to get the entire population vaccinated, and these doctors were jeopardizing that objective. Therefore, threats and character assassinations were immediately launched against them by the authorities and the media. This should have made everyone extremely suspicious, because what possible reason could anyone have for attacking doctors who were making people well? But once you have a general idea of what 2020 was all about, it gets easier to see who the good guys and the bad guys are, and the entire nonsensical mess begins to make perfect sense.

This chapter wouldn't be complete without writing down a partial list of the ingredients in a vaccine. They are Thimerosal (mercury), aluminum, formaldehyde, animal cell tissue, and in some vaccines, human fetal cell tissue from aborted babies. Without even an iota of medical knowledge, a person may legitimately ask whether any of this belongs in a human body. But it is the last ingredient that is the most disturbing to many Christians.

The medical mouthpieces for the pharmaceutical industry always try to give the public the impression that every qualified physician in the world supports the widespread use of vaccines. One of them was bold enough to state that vaccines are *settled science*. But since there are hundreds of thousands of very qualified physicians around the world who are either skeptical or opposed to vaccines, and since more are joining their ranks daily, I'd say the science is far from settled. Instead of being settled science, it would be more correct to say it's *settled propaganda.*

In addition, these propagandists have been using the same twisted logic for decades about vaccines, as we've heard about masks. Everyone must be vaccinated, so that they don't infect everyone else. But if their vaccines are as effective as they claim, then the only people anyone could possibly infect are those who have also exercised their God-given right not to be injected. They're fanatically promoting the injection of their magic potions into our bodies, even though according to them, those magic potions aren't effective unless everyone has them injected into *their* bodies. That doesn't remotely resemble the practice of medicine. It resembles sorcery, quackery, and cultism. They continuously spout such nonsense, they shamelessly lie about the harm vaccines have caused, they're terrified to debate the issue publicly, and they're pushing their magic potions on the public as if their livelihood depended on it. In all these ways, they have given themselves away and lost all credibility.

The globalists pretty much own Washington. They also own or control the medical establishment, the pharmaceutical industry, the internet platforms, and the mainstream media. It's a great scam this criminal gang has come up with, and by essentially owning all five of these power centers, the gang can do just about anything it wants to an unsuspecting public. When they get through fleecing the sheeple and destroying millions of lives through their vaccines, instead of looking like the villains they are, they will be hailed by many as heroes. They continually praise themselves through their own media outlets, and the blindest sheeple praise them as well. But the full story hasn't yet been written. People *are* waking up, and the first ones who have awakened are those whose lives have been destroyed by these peddlers of poisons. Their chilling words at the close of one very powerful documentary are that *one day, the entire world will know the truth about vaccines.*

THE GREATEST CON MAN IN THE WORLD

The globalists traffic in fear and they're constantly scaring up some kind of boogeyman. If it's not weapons of mass destruction, then it's terrorists. If it's not terrorists, then it's climate change. If it's not climate change, then it's a virus. There's no end to it, because their boogeyman department is open 24 hours a day, 365 days a year, in order to keep the sheeple in a perpetual state of fear. This is very important, because the more frightened sheeple are, the more obedient they are, and for what they've planned for humanity, the globalists need an awful lot of obedient sheeple.

The Lord tells us repeatedly in His Word, *fear not!* It should therefore be no surprise that Satan repeatedly tells people just the opposite. *Be afraid, be very afraid!* We don't need to look very far to discover who most people are listening to.

Those who are informed knew the very moment they saw the chapter title that it couldn't be about anyone else but Bill Gates. He stands head and shoulders above every con man who ever lived, and the world has had some great ones. One particularly gifted con man even managed to sell the Eiffel Tower for scrap metal to some gullible suckers. But for sheer audacity and for the magnitude of his cons, there's no one who even comes close to Bill Gates. Some of the main items he's been peddling since he began his operation are fear, viruses, pandemics, depopulation, digital IDs for tracking everyone on the planet, and the vehicle for that tracking, *vaccines!* The reason he needs to be exposed, is because unlike other con men who've taken the money and ran, he's taking the money and staying. He's working multiple cons on the whole world, while those he's bought off are applauding, and while the whole world is watching.

For those who may not know, the word *con* is short for confidence. A con man tries to gain people's confidence, so that they would let down their guard and allow the scoundrel to take them for everything they have. The better the con man, the more confidence he can inspire in people. Bill Gates is a pitiful example of a con man, in the sense that he doesn't really inspire a lot of confidence. Many people who hear him talk become instantly wary, because there's an obvious kind of fakeness and creepiness about him. If he was a two-bit con man working the streets, he'd starve to death. But he's got three things that the average con man doesn't have. An unlimited amount of money, free access into everyone's home through television, and a huge network of front organizations and media outlets, all continually praising him for his charitable work on behalf of humanity. With resources like that, even the most despicable reprobate can be made to look like a saint.

An article appeared in the *Columbia Journalism Review* on August 21, 2020, that sheds light on how the Bill and Melinda Gates Foundation (worth over 46 billion dollars) influences media reporting. Here's a small excerpt from that very revealing article: *"I* *recently examined nearly twenty thousand charitable grants the Gates Foundation had made through the end of June and found more than $250 million going toward journalism. Recipients included news operations like the BBC, NBC, Al Jazeera, ProPublica, National Journal, The Guardian, Univision, Medium, the Financial Times, The Atlantic, the Texas Tribune, Gannett, Washington Monthly, Le Monde, and the Center for Investigative Reporting; charitable organizations affiliated with news outlets, like BBC Media Action and the New York Times' Neediest Cases Fund"…."the National Press Foundation, and the International Center for Journalists."*

GAVI, the Global Alliance for Vaccination and Immunization, an offshoot of the Gates Foundation has already spent $15 billion promoting vaccines and making friends. When you hear Bill Gates praised from every quarter, it isn't necessarily because people have any great love for him, but they do have great love for his money. Proverbs 19:6 gives a perfect insight into the good press phenomenon of Bill Gates and other globalists. *"Many will entreat the favor of a generous man, And every man is a friend to him who gives gifts."*

Philanthropy is the greatest cover for villainy ever devised, and the globalists are passionate about it. Whether it's $10 million for a shelter for abused animals, or $100 million to feed starving children in Africa, they can always be counted on to lend a helping hand. Whatever the cause, whatever the charity, whatever the need, their checkbooks are out in a flash, and they never fail to save the day. With as much philanthropy as they're continually involved in, you would think they would pretty soon go broke. But the truth is that it doesn't cost them a cent. All their charitable contributions to noble causes are written off their taxes, and at worst, they end up breaking even. Sometimes when they set up foundations, trusts or charities, because of massive conflicts of interest and various financial manipulations, they actually end up *making money.* Bill Gates is a master at using philanthropy as a cover. The $250 million that went to media outlets is a drop in the bucket compared to the billions the Gates Foundation has been funneling into a multitude of charities. Everywhere his money reaches, Bill Gates can count on having friends, and all those friends can't praise him enough. The multitude whose lives Bill Gates has destroyed are never sought out by the media for comment. The media turns *them* into villains!

The gullible fall for the philanthropy aspect of the con, because in their minds, anyone who gives billions to charity must have a kind heart. So, let's take a look at some of the things Bill Gates has said and done, and you can judge for yourself how kind his heart is.

The Bill and Melinda Gates Foundation is one of the greatest self-promotion and influence peddling operations ever created. Far from breaking Bill Gates, it has allowed him to more than double his net worth in about 10 years. A decade ago, his net worth was estimated to be about $54 billion. Today, that number is more than $130 billion. Philanthropy seems to be an extremely lucrative enterprise. Bill Gates has investments in various ventures, but the one that accounts for most of his wealth is vaccines. In 2010, he named the coming decade *"the decade of vaccines,"* and almost single-handed ensured that it would become just that. The Gates Foundation is the number one contributor to the World Health Organization, having pumped billions into it. From its inception, the WHO has been the leading proponent of mass vaccinations, and due to his massive contributions to the organization, Bill Gates now practically runs it. Over the years, the

Gates Foundation has also pumped billions into various hospitals and medical institutions that promote vaccination, and that come up with favorable vaccination studies. It has pumped over $150 million into the CDC alone.

Most people think the CDC is nothing more than an independent public health agency. No possible connection to the globalists, and no conflicts of interest. Those who hold this view should listen to the words of Robert F. Kennedy Jr. The following comes from an interview he did with RT America:

"The CDC is actually a vaccine company. The CDC has a total budget of about 11 billion dollars a year. It spends five billion of that buying vaccines from those four companies....making sweetheart deals that are much higher. Where we pay with taxpayer money much more for the vaccines than they pay for the exact same vaccine in Europe. Then they distribute those vaccines to the American public. So, they're approving the vaccine, they're mandating them for the public, they're buying them from these companies who they're friends with. And then they're, they're basically forcing 78 million people to take an untested product. The CDC also owns patents on many of the vaccines, in fact across HHS, which is the mother agency. FDA, CDC and NIH, which all regulate vaccines, different parts of the vaccine industry, are all parts of HHS, and those agencies are allowed to hold patents on the vaccines that their scientists work on, and then collect royalties. And in fact, officials in those agencies, who worked on the vaccines, can also own part of the patent and collect royalties of up to $150,000 a year. So, every bottle of Gardasil that is sold, HHS is making money on it. They make tens of millions of dollars a year. So, you have the regulatory agency actually making money, by pushing and mandating

this vaccine to people, and then collecting money on it, and ignoring the health effects when people are injured. And these are zero liability products, no matter how toxic the ingredient, no matter how grievous your injury, no matter how negligent the company. You can't sue them. They can do anything they want with a vaccine, and you can't do anything about it."

When Covid showed up, Bill Gates looked like a hungry wolf that had just spotted a stray sheep. When the reported death toll from the virus in America was only a few hundred, he knew beyond any doubt that the crisis could only be managed with vaccines, and he took advantage of every opportunity to send that message to the world:

"For the world at large, normalcy only returns when we've largely vaccinated the entire global population." TV interview with Financial Times, April 9, 2020

As mentioned earlier, Bill Gates is heavily invested in the development of digital technology to track people. Every once in a while, he opens his mouth and says more about it than he should. When that happens and there's a firestorm, the professional liars and the globalist fronts masquerading as fact-checkers go into full-scale attack mode against anyone who simply calls attention to Bill Gates' own words. Words such as these:

"Eventually we will have some digital certificates to show who has recovered or been tested recently or when we have a vaccine who has received it." Redditt AMA, March 18, 2020

Like every other globalist, Bill Gates has a very casual and flippant way about him when talking about other human beings. It is as if every person on earth has been put here only for his private experiments. Here's a quote from an interview in Brussels some years ago:

"We are taking things that are genetically-modified organisms and injecting them into little kids' arms, we just shoot 'em right into the vein."

Besides vaccinating everyone on the planet and putting some kind of a tracking device on every man, woman, and child, perhaps Bill Gates' greatest passion is reducing the world's population. He rarely opens his mouth without this pet project of his coming up. But the Lord told people to be *fruitful and multiply,* and He made our planet large enough and rich enough to accommodate a much greater population than the current one. It's true that large cities are overpopulated, but if one drives across the country, one sees mostly empty spaces. Since God made Himself abundantly clear on this issue, it shouldn't be too difficult to figure out from whom the idea of depopulating the world comes from. Here's what Bill Gates had to say about it in 2010:

"The world has 6.8 billion people. That's headed up to about 9 billion. Now, if we do a really great job on vaccines, health care, reproductive health services, we could lower that by perhaps 10 to 15 percent."

Bill Gates took some heat for this comment. Not so much for the idea of depopulation, but about how that was to be achieved.

He has spent huge amounts of money on public relations firms, who have tried to sanitize these words and convince everyone that he didn't really mean what he said. These firms and the many lying fact-checkers have gone to great lengths to essentially change the meaning of words. When you listen to their convoluted explanations, you'll conclude that we longer have a need for dictionaries, because there's no way of ever really knowing what any word means.

The pharmaceutical companies and Bill Gates have realized that vaccines are a very lucrative business. Especially since it doesn't involve any liability issues. A few years ago, Bill Gates told us just how lucrative the vaccine business is:

"We see a phenomenal track record. It's been a $100 billion overall that the world's put in, our foundation it's a bit more than $10 billion. But we feel there's been over a 20 to 1 return. So, if you just look at the economic benefits, that's a pretty strong number compared to anything else."

As stated earlier, Robert F. Kennedy Jr. is an advocate for those harmed by vaccines, as well as an outspoken critic of the pharmaceutical industry. He's also no fan of Bill Gates, and on April 9, 2020, he posted a scathing exposé of the vaccine peddler on Instagram. It's somewhat lengthy, but it's well worth reading. My apologies to Robert Kennedy for any transcription errors. Here's the real truth about Bill Gates and his vaccines:

"Vaccines, for Bill Gates, are a strategic philanthropy that feed his many vaccine-related businesses (including Microsoft's ambition

to control a global vac ID enterprise) and give him dictatorial control over global health policy – the spear tip of corporate neo-imperialism.

Gates' obsession with vaccines seems fueled by a messianic conviction that he is ordained to save the world with technology and a god-like willingness to experiment with the lives of lesser humans.

Promising to eradicate Polio with $1.2 billion, Gates took control of India's National Advisory Board (NAB) and mandated 50 polio vaccines (up from 5) to every child before age 5. Indian doctors blame the Gates campaign for a devastating vaccine-strain polio epidemic that paralyzed 496,000 children between 2000 and 2017. In 2017, the Indian Government dialed back Gates' vaccine regimen and evicted Gates and his cronies from the NAB. Polio paralysis rates dropped precipitously. In 2017, the World Health Organization reluctantly admitted that the global polio explosion is predominantly vaccine strain, meaning it is coming from Gates' Vaccine Program. The most frightening epidemics in Congo, the Philippines, and Afghanistan are all linked to Gates' vaccines. By 2018, ¾ of global polio cases were from Gates' vaccines.

In 2014, the Gates Foundation funded tests of experimental HPV vaccines, developed by GSK and Merck, on 23,000 young girls in remote Indian provinces. Approximately 1,200 suffered severe side effects, including autoimmune and fertility disorders. Seven died. Indian government investigations charged that Gates funded researchers committed pervasive ethical violations: pressuring vulnerable village girls into the trial, bullying parents, forging consent forms, and refusing medical care to the injured girls.

In 2010, the Gates Foundation funded a trial of a GSK's experimental malaria vaccine, killing 151 African infants and causing serious adverse effects including paralysis, seizure, and febrile convulsions to 1,048 of the 5,049 children.

During Gates 2002 MenAfriVac Campaign in Sub-Saharan Africa, Gates operatives forcibly vaccinated thousands of African children against meningitis. Between 50-500 children developed paralysis. South African newspapers complained, 'we are guinea pigs for drug makers.'

Nelson Mandela's former Senior Economist, Professor Patrick Bond, describes Gates' philanthropic practices as 'ruthless' and 'immoral.'

In 2010, Gates committed $10 billion to the WHO promising to reduce population, in part, through new vaccines. A month later Gates told a Ted Talk that new vaccines 'could reduce population.' In 2014, Kenya's Catholic Doctors Association accused the WHO of chemically sterilizing millions of unwilling Kenyan women with a phony 'tetanus' vaccine campaign. Independent labs found the sterility formula in every vaccine tested. After denying the charges, WHO finally admitted it had been developing the sterility vaccines for over a decade.

Similar accusations came from Tanzania, Nicaragua, Mexico and the Philippines.

A 2017 study (Morgensen et.AI.2017) showed that WHO's popular DTP is killing more Africans than the disease it pretends to prevent. Vaccinated girls suffered 10x the death rate of unvaccinated children.

Gates and the WHO refused to recall the lethal vaccine which WHO forces upon millions of African children annually.

Global public health advocates around the world accuse Gates of hijacking WHO's agenda away from the projects that are proven to curb infectious diseases; clean water, hygiene, nutrition and economic development. They say he has diverted agency resources to serve his personal fetish – that good health only comes in a syringe.

In addition to using his philanthropy to control WHO, UNICEF, GAVI and PATH, Gates funds private pharmaceutical companies that manufacture vaccines, and a massive network of pharmaceutical industry front groups that broadcast deceptive propaganda, develop fraudulent studies, conduct surveillance and psychological operations against vaccine hesitancy and use Gates' power and money to silence dissent and coerce compliance.

In his recent nonstop Pharmedia appearances, Gates appears gleeful that the Covid-19 crisis will give him the opportunity to force his third-world vaccine programs on American children."

How often have we heard our elected officials say that this or that law is being passed *"for the children"?* Our media friends always eagerly take up the chant, and every channel we turn to, we hear it's *"for the children."* But after reading Robert Kennedy's post, how many of our elected representatives and TV "journalists" do you think care one whit about the children? Regarding what you've just read, I haven't heard a peep out of any of them. On the contrary, their chorus of praise for Bill Gates is never-ending.

But it gets much worse when it comes to covering up the criminal activities of Bill Gates. Instagram has banned Robert Kennedy from its platform, in large part because of the post you've just read. How did they justify banning him? One of their spokespersons had this to say: *"We removed this account for repeatedly sharing debunked claims about the coronavirus or vaccines."* I would assume from this quote that Instagram is making the claim that the facts Robert Kennedy presented are not facts at all, but are just stories he made up. But that can't be, because all he has said is well documented and can be easily verified, so what is Instagram saying when they talk about debunked claims? They're essentially saying that if they pronounce something as debunked, then even without providing a shred of evidence in support of such a pronouncement, it *is* debunked! In other comments they've made about banning Robert Kennedy from their platform, they've asserted that the facts he presented might lead people to distrust vaccines. In other words, they're saying people should not have a right to find out about a product that has crippled and killed thousands, or perhaps even millions, because if they did, they might not wish to use that product. It's difficult to wrap your mind around this line of reasoning, because what they're essentially saying is that they *want* people to use a product that has crippled or killed multitudes, so that they won't miss out on the opportunity to be crippled or killed themselves! This is not only deranged, this is downright *criminal!*

There are a couple serious issues here. First of all, by censoring truth tellers like Robert Kennedy for exposing actual crimes, these people are complicit in a criminal cover-up. For this, they should be prosecuted to the full extent of the law. Secondly, if people should suffer grievous injuries or die because of their actions, they should be prosecuted for that as well. We have seen way too much of this type of lawlessness in recent years, and unless there are guaranteed serious consequences, such lawlessness *will* continue.

In conclusion, please consider the fact that Bill Gates is not a doctor, or an epidemiologist, or a virologist, and is therefore in no way qualified to dispense medical advice or medical care. Nevertheless, he has granted himself the authority to determine health policy for me, you, your loved ones, our nation, and the entire world! Bill Gates has less medical training than a first-year med school student, yet he is invited to speak on all the mainstream news outlets, to leaders of governments, and is being deferred to everywhere he speaks as the world's leading authority on health! He determines world health policy, now wishes to mandate that policy, having invested at least $10 billion dollars into that policy! Doesn't this entire scenario seem utterly bizarre? Please correct me if I'm wrong, but the last I heard, practicing medicine without a license was illegal. If I heard right, then just how illegal are the actions of Bill Gates, and why does the law not apply to him?

A petition was sent to the White House in April of 2020, which calls for "Investigations into the 'Bill and Melinda Gates Foundation' for Medical Malpractice & Crimes Against Humanity." It currently has over 689,000 signatures. Bill Gates is clearly a menace to our society and to the world at large, but the problem isn't just one man. The problem is a sinister globalist agenda that is enriching and empowering a few, at the expense of everyone else.

THE MAINSTREAM MEDIA

There's an old saying almost everyone has heard. *Fool me once, shame on you, fool me twice, shame on me.* How about, *fool me a thousand times?* Whose shame would that be? I suppose in that case, *both* parties should feel a *lot* of shame. In later chapters, we'll deal with those who have been systematically lied to for years, and have practically begged to be lied to some more. In this chapter, we'll deal with the liars.

The mainstream media can be divided into two parts, news and entertainment. Many working for the mainstream media have been very naughty boys and girls. It's difficult to know whether the news or the entertainment kids deserve the bigger spanking. I'll therefore try to be even-handed, so nobody feels left out.

We all love entertainment. Life would be pretty dull without it, but there's a huge difference between entertainment and propaganda. Much of what we call news in today's America is really just propaganda, and the same can be said about our national entertainment. It's less about stirring our emotions, making us laugh, cry or feel joy, and more about pounding alien ideas into our heads. The same agendas that are constantly being pushed by the news kids, are constantly on the lips of the entertainment kids.

Ordinary Americans think and talk about ordinary things, but not this bunch. Most of them are a walking, talking commercial, on and off the camera, for everything the globalists espouse.

Just like the news side, the entertainment side is big on the promotion of certain bizarre terms that have mysteriously crept into our vocabulary. Terms like *"conspiracy theory," "the new normal," "social distancing," "white privilege," "politically correct,"* and perhaps the most dangerous one of all, *"hate speech."* These terms have been designed for two specific purposes. To enforce mindless conformity, and to cause division among the people.

In places like Communist China, North Korea or Nazi Germany, the terms *"politically correct"* and *"hate speech"* would be completely appropriate. In those places, there could only be one correct way to think and one correct way to speak. But such terms have no place in a free society. What makes a free society free is precisely the fact that everyone is free to think and speak any way one chooses. The use of perverted terms like *"politically correct"* and *"hate speech"* is an open admission by a society that it is no longer free.

It's no coincidence that *"politically correct"* came first, and *"hate speech"* came later. When turning a free society into a dictatorship, the social engineering and mind control must follow a logical progression. It must also be done gradually. Doing it too fast would be like dropping the frog into a boiling pot of water. The frog might wake up to the danger and jump out, which is the last thing tyrants want.

The American people have had numerous warnings, over a very long period of time, that the water was getting hotter. The appearance of the term *"politically correct"* was a huge one, and at that point there still may have been time for the frog to jump out of the pot. When the term *"hate speech"* appeared, and began to be widely used and accepted, the frog was nearly cooked.

The media first began telling the American people that we must all think a certain way, and once that took hold, it began telling us that we must all talk a certain way. What most Americans never bothered to ask is, who exactly is deciding how we should think and talk? And they also never bothered to ask by what right anyone is making such decisions? Just like the frog in the pot, the American people didn't notice the water getting hotter, as more and more nonsense was being pounded into our heads. The nonsense gained credibility, as more and more media personalities got on the bandwagon. The incentive for them was obvious from the start. Money and fame.

The term *"hate speech"* needs a little clarification. Whenever it's employed, it's not really referring to hateful speech, but to a *particular type of speech.* For example, atheists, God-haters, and Bible mockers can say the most vile and hateful things about God, Jesus Christ, the Bible, and Christians. That's perfectly acceptable, and even praiseworthy. What absolutely cannot be tolerated and must be censored, is even the mildest criticism of Satan and all his works. The next time you hear the term *"hate speech"* being used by those who love that term, please notice how hateful and intolerant *their* speech is. Eradicating hate is the very last thing they want, because they live and breathe hate. Their two main objectives are to silence anyone who doesn't share their godless ideology, and to shove that ideology down everyone's throat.

Bashing Christians and the Judeo-Christian worldview, as well as pushing globalist agendas, has become a financial bonanza and all the naughty boys and girls want a piece of the pie. If you want that coveted movie role, it helps to support leftist causes. If you want immediate funding for a movie project, it helps if it has a *"politically correct"* message. If you want a recording contract, it helps to sing the kind of songs the globalists like. If you want an anchor slot on the TV news, it helps to be a God-hater and a liar. That's not to say the naughty boys and girls weren't *already* naughty. The promise of money and fame however, has made them much, much naughtier.

They all try to outdo each other in being *"politically correct,"* because they all know that's where the bread is buttered. The entertainment kids can be somewhat excused for being uninformed or brainwashed about important issues, and for generally having their heads in the clouds. As everyone knows, Hollywood and all other entertainment venues are awash in drugs, parties, and a reality that is completely disconnected from the reality of ordinary Americans. What is more difficult to overlook is their blatant hatred for the Bible and for Jesus Christ.

When late night talk show hosts and Hollywood celebrities mock the multitude of charlatans on TV who pretend to be preachers of the Gospel, I don't have any problem with that. They should be mocked, and the sooner they're off the air the better. All they do is give the Lord and those who love Him a bad name. What is inexcusable however, are their insults and blasphemies against Jesus Christ. Please consider the fact that Jesus is the kindest, gentlest, and most loving person who ever lived. He is the very essence of goodness and perfection, and when He challenged his enemies to point out a single sin in Him, even those who hated Him the most couldn't do it. For close to 2,000 years, no one has been able to do it!

So, what's the problem with the naughty kids in the entertainment media? Why do they seem to feel the need to endlessly mock Jesus, while fawning over every reprobate? Please notice that the one thing you never, ever see them doing is insulting any other religious leader, or any pagan god. If they tried the most innocent of jokes on Buddha, Mohamed, Confucius, Allah or Shiva, they'd be out on their ear and there would be a target on their backs. They think their religious mockery makes them look tough, but since it only goes as far as Jesus, they are demonstrating that they're nothing but gutless cowards. Perhaps this can be better understood when you look at the hand gestures of many celebrities. When appearing on magazine covers or any time there's a camera around, they're almost always gesturing with their hands. They flash many hand signs, but some of the more popular are the devil's horns, the Satanic pyramid, the circle over one eye with three fingers sticking up, symbolizing 666, the hidden hand of Freemasonry, and covering one eye with a hand or some object, symbolizing the all-seeing eye of Lucifer. They're not shy in the least about telling the world who they serve.

Since many of the Hollywood crowd practice various forms of sexual deviancy, it should come as no surprise that Hollywood is continually promoting it. For example, while homosexuals comprise at maximum about 3% of the population, homosexual characters show up in vastly larger numbers in sit-coms, movies, and everywhere else. Furthermore, they are almost always portrayed in the best possible light. They are kind, loving, funny, generous, honest, noble, and open-minded. Christian characters on the other hand, are almost always portrayed as hateful, bigoted, narrow-minded creeps. Hollywood has been promoting deviant lifestyles and smearing Christians in this way for decades. All those involved know that all this constitutes blatant deception. They also know that stirring up hate and division can produce nothing but harm to our society, but this does not dissuade them in the least. They consider themselves much more enlightened than mere mortals like us, and are quite proud of what they're doing.

The naughty kids in the news media are no better when it comes to deceiving the public and stirring up hate. To say that their reporting is biased doesn't begin to describe their countless deceptions. There are many ways to deceive the public. The simplest way is to flat out lie. An example of this would be telling people that this or that has been debunked, when they know full well that the only things that have been debunked are their ridiculous, fact-free narratives. A very simple way to discredit all so-called, supposedly debunked "conspiracy theories," would be to have a free and open discussion about all controversial issues on their news channels. Just invite the "crazy conspiracy theorists" to some debate forum and make fools of them in front of the entire nation. They can't do this however, because if they ever did, *they're* the ones who would end up looking like fools.

I do understand the predicament they're in. They're working at places where what they can and can't say is prescribed for them, and if they deviate from the official narrative, there's a good chance they'll be fired. We've all witnessed what happened to Tucker Carlson. So, they only have three options. One option is to hide in their studios and lie like the devil to get their paycheck. The second option is to grow a backbone and speak the truth regardless of the consequences. And the third option is to walk away from a job that requires them to lie on a daily basis. From what I'm seeing, just about all of them have chosen the first option.

Another very common method the media uses to deceive people is to over-emphasize certain stories while ignoring others. Because of this particular deception, we have a totally distorted view of the world. An example of this is to give one side of a controversial issue way more coverage than another, which happens constantly with the abortion controversy and the LGBTQ controversy. When half a million pro-life supporters show up at a yearly rally in Washington DC, don't send a single reporter or a single cameraman to cover it. But when a couple dozen pro-choice protesters show up at a state capitol during the consideration of a heartbeat bill, ABC, NBC, CBS, CNN, MSNBC, and Fox must all be there. When there's a pro-traditional family rally at a stadium and 35,000 people show up, don't interview a single one of them. But be sure to interview the dozen protesters outside. Is it any wonder that public opinion on these and many other issues has been changing precisely the way the globalists want? That of course is entirely the point of such deceptions.

In the past, journalism used to be an honorable profession, but many of today's "journalists" have completely disgraced it. Most people have heard the old joke about how to tell when a politician is lying. The answer for those who haven't heard the joke: *When his lips are moving.* The same joke can be made today about most of those who pretend to be journalists. The great majority of them are no longer reporting the news, but pushing propaganda. It may be shocking to hear, but news coverage in today's America is not all that different from news coverage in China. It has very little to do with informing the public, and has everything to do with enshrining official government narratives and brutally browbeating dissenters.

The 5 W's of journalism are what, who, when, where, and why. Most of today's journalists, reporters, and commentators barely pass with the first four W's, because they devote most of their time to mundane trivialities, and almost completely ignore what's important. When they get to the fifth W, it's almost a certainty that you'll get a good dose of propaganda. An example of this might be a school shooting. Every time one happens, you can count on hearing endless drivel about the easy availability of guns, and the need for stricter background checks and stricter gun laws. But what you will almost never hear is anything about the glamorizing of violence and bloodshed through violent movies, violent video games, and violent lyrics in some popular music. You also won't hear anything about the removal of prayer, the Bible, and the Ten Commandments from schools. Also conspicuously absent will be any mention of the breakdown of the nuclear family, permissiveness and lack of discipline on the part of parents, and the general godless state of our society. The tendency of the journalists, reporters, and commentators is to blame anything and everything, *except* the misguided choices of our society. Most of them go to great lengths to convince the public that the magic solution to every societal problem is more government control, even though this is precisely what has caused most of the problems.

The layout of an average newspaper is an example of how legitimate journalism is supposed to work. World, national, and local news are all called hard news. What follows is called soft news. There are only two sections of the paper that are reserved for commentary and opinion. The opinion section, and to a much lesser extent, the lifestyle section. All the rest should be straight facts reporting. So, is this how news is being reported today? All one needs to do is turn on the TV news, to see that whether it's hard news, soft news, business, sports, politics, lifestyle, the entire gamut is nothing but continual commentary and opinion. That is not journalism, that is a farce and an utter disgrace.

In the major newspapers that are owned or controlled by the globalists, the reporting is as bad or even worse. Not only is commentary and opinion running throughout the hard news section, but sometimes even the headlines are commentary. It's not uncommon to see headlines like these: *Quack Doctors Descend On Washington* (a story about America's Frontline Doctors), or *Misleading And Discredited PLANDEMIC Documentary Pulled By Sinclair Broadcasting.* There's no end to such headlines, and when we see them, the alarm bells should immediately go off, because no legitimate headline would ever be written like that.

The Bible says the following in the book of Proverbs 12:22: *"Lying lips are an abomination to the Lord."* Lying is not only abhorrent to God, but it's also one of the most dangerous sins, because unlike many other sins, it almost always multiplies. While very bad, idolatry, blasphemy, theft or murder can be committed once, and never be committed again. This is generally not so with lying. Every lie, more often than not, leads to more lies to cover up the original, and those in turn lead to even more lies. This domino effect must eventually bury the liar. Detectives have caught many criminals, simply because they could no longer keep their stories straight. America's mainstream media deceivers have created the same predicament for themselves, and as a result, today their lying house of cards is beginning to collapse.

I already mentioned that the deceivers won't permit free and open discussion about a host of controversial issues about which they're flat out lying. That of course is a dead giveaway. Another dead giveaway is them continually attacking truth tellers. Over the years, they've invented all kinds of derogatory labels, and they pin them on any truth tellers they wish to discredit. Here are a few of their inventions: *"anti-masker," "anti-vaxxer," "truther," "racist," "sexist," "homophobe," transphobe," "bigot," "right-wing extremist," "white supremacist," "fascist," "science-denier,"* and perhaps the most popular one of all, *"crazy conspiracy theorist."* If you hear anyone throwing these labels around like confetti, you can be certain you're listening to a liar. Name-calling, deflection, misdirection, and flat out lying are just some of the tricks the news media has been using to deceive the American people for a very long time. Unfortunately, their silly little tricks have been extraordinarily effective for a very long time, because it seems that our nation has no shortage of the gullible.

In summation, today's news media operates much like a religious cult. Almost all the faces we see on the screen are the cult leadership, and they never cease telling us that *only they* possess the ultimate truth about every issue. They practically forbid people to think for themselves and to consider alternative viewpoints, labeling every deviation from the official narrative *"dangerous misinformation."* This is music to the ears of the sheeple. They know that thinking for oneself is a very heavy burden to bear, and they're greatly relieved to have our media friends sacrificially bear that burden for us. Even the most brainwashed sheeple could be deprogrammed quite easily, if they simply disobeyed the cult leaders and exposed themselves to the *"dangerous misinformation"* they're always being warned about. But unfortunately, most of them will never do it. Many have been so well trained, they won't even watch a ten-minute video that the cult leaders have labeled *"dangerous misinformation."* One misguided and frightened soul admitted to me, *"I'd rather not know the truth."* That's the kind of power this cult possesses.

Many players are responsible for unleashing destruction on the country we love, but perhaps none more so than the naughty boys and girls in the mainstream media. Their endless deceptions and cover-ups have led the nation down the path of confusion and darkness, and made the disaster of 2020 possible. They became famous and made piles of money, but their reckless actions practically ensured that there would be no future for their children and their grandchildren. They unleashed a tsunami of destruction that hasn't yet fully hit our shores, *but it's coming!*

All the players who have assisted in the destruction of countless lives and of America, will one day have to give an account for their actions. Perhaps not to the American people, but to the Judge of all the earth who is patiently waiting for them.

PART THREE:

THE CONCLUSION

A NATION UNDER
DIVINE JUDGMENT

I have some good news and some bad news. First, the bad news: America has in all likelihood crossed the point of no return, in which case the only direction from here is down. Now, the good news: Not every American needs to go down with the ship.

All nations go through six stages. The birth stage, the growth stage, the Golden Age, the decline, depravity, and destruction. 2020 was the beginning of the destruction stage for America, and I wish to share in a very abbreviated way how we got there.

Much can be said about the first two stages of America's timeline, but for our purposes, I'll summarize. People lived on this continent long before the first Europeans arrived, but there was no cohesive civilization. It was a tribal and splintered society. All of that changed however, when the first European settlers arrived in the early 1600's. They brought with them a book, which they planned to use as a guide for building a new society. That book was the Bible.

These early settlers were far from perfect. Just like us, they were flawed in every way, and struggled to navigate the maze of life. But they had a lantern to guide them, the very Word of God.

It was upon this Word that they founded a nation, and as we know, that nation thrived. Except for Israel, no other nation in history has experienced the abundance of blessings that America has.

As stated earlier, following the Revolutionary War, the founding fathers used the Bible to structure the government and to form our justice system. This reliance on the Word of God in governing ourselves brought unprecedented prosperity to the new nation. There was only one problem. Many of the rights guaranteed to every citizen were routinely being denied to one segment of the population. Black people had very few rights, and some had no rights at all. Some were considered property.

The Lord promises in His Word that He would bless a nation that honors Him, and to the extent that America honored the Lord, He kept His promise. The other side of the coin is the promise to punish a nation that dishonors Him, and this He also did. When America dishonored the Lord with the abomination of slavery, our nation was punished with the Civil War. Some who are Biblically illiterate believe that the Bible actually approves of slavery, but nothing could be further from the truth. The indentured servitude which the Bible talks about bears no resemblance to the slavery that led to the Civil War. The kidnapping of people, the buying and selling of people, and the abuse of people are all things that God's Word condemns in the strongest of terms. Having said that, because of the extreme nature of the evil that some in America practiced and which our society tolerated too long, the Lord imposed an extremely severe punishment on the entire nation. Estimates vary, but about 700,000 lives were lost in the Civil War, by far the bloodiest war in our nation's history. This should make it abundantly clear that when the Lord speaks, He is always to be taken seriously.

I've heard it said that the Civil War was about states' rights rather than slavery, but it seems to me that this is a distinction without a difference. The issue of states' rights could apply to any number of things, but what sparked the Civil War was the fact that the federal government encroached upon states' rights in regard to the issue of *slavery*. It's difficult to imagine any other states' rights issue generating enough passion to cause brother to kill brother.

Please allow me to state at the very outset that I have no great love for either of the two major political parties. Both have done their very best to run America completely into the ground, and the place they've brought us to, there's almost no coming back from. But in the context of slavery and racism, the Democrat Party deserves a special mention. From its inception in 1829, the Democrat Party was a pro-slavery Party. The Republican Party on the other hand, was founded in 1854 as an anti-slavery Party.

In the 1857 Dredd Scott case, the Supreme Court ruled that slaves weren't citizens but property. The seven Justices who voted in favor were all Democrats, and the two dissenting Justices were Republicans. The 13th Amendment of 1865 which abolished slavery was opposed by Democrats. The 14th Amendment of 1866 which gave blacks citizenship was opposed by Democrats. The 15th Amendment of 1869 which gave blacks voting rights was opposed by Democrats. All three passed only because of universal Republican support.

The founder of the Ku Klux Klan, Nathan Bedford Forrest, was a Democrat. From its inception, almost all members of the KKK have been Democrats. Professor Eric Foner, who was himself a Democrat, had this to say about the KKK: *"In effect, the Klan was a military force serving the interests of the Democratic Party."*

Following the Civil War, a reign of terror began in the south against freed slaves, and it was orchestrated by Democrats. There were murders, rapes, and arson, and this continued until well into the 20th century. Democrats passed oppressive laws that kept blacks from voting or owning businesses, and they imposed racial segregation. Finally, the majority of Democrats opposed the Civil Rights Acts of the 1960's.

The reason I've said all this, is because the American people need to know their own history, so they won't believe every con artist or fall for every scam that comes along. Today, many prominent Democrats love to label their opponents racist, but when we consider the abominable history of the Democrat Party, for *any* Democrat to call *anyone* a racist is on par with the town drunk preaching about the evils of alcohol and passing out fliers for AA meetings!

When it comes to the issue of race, there's an awful lot of heat, but very little light. The race hustlers, agitators, and media provocateurs need to be exposed for the liars and self-righteous hypocrites they are. They could talk for years, and never mention many important facts about America's history. *The first, is that about 300,000 Union soldiers, most of whom were white, voluntarily laid down their lives to free their black brothers and sisters! The second, is that millions of white people voluntarily sacrificed their own sons, fathers, brothers, and uncles to bring about the end of slavery!* There are many other relevant facts that the con artists deliberately omit, so that they can continue to spread their lying narrative and hate. However, based on these two facts alone, isn't it high time that all of them shut their mouths and stop inciting people to violence?

I regret having to use the words *"white"* and *"black"* when discussing this issue. All our lives we've been told that people are white, black, red, and yellow, and it's unfortunate that we've been taught to communicate in those terms. The truth of the matter is that all people are simply a *different shade of brown*, and there exists only one race of people in the world, *the human race.*

Whether it's skin shade, masks, vaccines, and countless other issues, the American people have been cleverly and diabolically manipulated to turn on each other. There's a very good reason why the globalists wanted the Bible out of the schools. It contains many pearls of wisdom, which smooth talking tyrants and con artists hope we never see. One such pearl can be found in Proverbs 14:15, which says *"The naive believes everything."* If people knew just this Bible verse and gave it serious thought, the myriad of lies and nutty ideas that our society is drowning in would have been flatly rejected. If we were as Biblically literate as the generation of the founding fathers, there's an excellent chance we would still have all our God-given rights.

At the end of World War II, America gained superpower status and entered its Golden Age. Less than 20 years later, the Golden Age was over, and the decline began. The 1960's generation was the catalyst for that decline. They were the first generation indoctrinated by the talking box, which confirmed everything they were being taught in school. One of the things they were being taught was that evolution was true, which of course meant that the Bible was not. The movie *Inherit the Wind* was released right around that time, and it cemented the brainwashing. This generation was more privileged than any which came before, because they were born in the richest nation of all time, during its Golden Age. All these factors made them hugely arrogant, and consequently they turned their backs on God.

When a society turns its back on God, some questions need to be answered. For instance, if God no longer decides what's right or wrong, then who does? The obvious answer is that *we do,* but there's a slight problem with that. God is one and we are many, so, which of us gets to decide? The answer to that is obvious as well, *we all do.* This is where Socialism and chaos enter the picture.

Once God is removed as the arbiter of truth and morality, then man automatically becomes the arbiter of both. We hear a lot of people today say things like *"your truth is your truth and my truth is my truth."* This is much like what we find in the book of Judges 21:25, where it says *"everyone did what was right in his own eyes."* The chaos we see in America today is the inevitable result of this type of thinking.

Before the huge cultural shift of the 1960's, there was a general consensus about what was right and wrong. Since that time however, it has been a free for all when it comes to every issue. The debates are heated and there's no way to resolve *any* issue, because once the Law of God is rejected, there's no legitimate basis to claim that anyone is any more right than anyone else. Everyone has their own truth after all.

Our founding fathers had a great challenge before them following the Revolutionary War. They had to form a government, but what kind? A number of ideas were proposed, and after much heated debate, they finally settled on a representative Constitutional Republic. One idea that was proposed was a Democracy, but it was quickly scrapped, because the founders knew that majority rule was nothing more than mob rule. The kind of government the founders gave us is one where the people *do* have a say, but *only* within the framework of the Constitution, in which certain foundational principles overrule even the will of the majority.

Biblical morality started to erode in the 1960's, and since the foundational principles of the Constitution are based on the Law of God, they started to erode as well. The decline was underway, and it was greatly aided by one particular judgment of God, which is described for us in the first chapter of the book of Romans.

The Lord judges nations in various ways. Sometimes He withholds blessings such as rainfall, sometimes He appoints wicked rulers over wicked people, and sometimes He allows foreign armies to invade. But there is one judgment of God that is distinctive from all the rest. The three-part judgment of abandonment. This judgment occurs when the Lord turns His back on a society or a nation, and it is perhaps the most severe judgment of all.

All people have the general revelation of God through creation, and some have the special revelation of His written Word. But whatever the extent of the revelation, all nations and all people are accountable to the Lord for the light that they *do* have. If nations or individuals respond positively to the light they have, the Lord will *always* grant more light. If the light is continually rejected, at God's appointed time, the judgment of abandonment descends upon a nation. This is what happened to America in the 1960's. America turned its back on God, and God turned His back on America.

A full explanation of God's abandonment of nations can be found in the book of Romans 1:18-23:

"For the wrath of God is revealed from heaven against all ungodliness and unrighteousness of men, who suppress the truth in unrighteousness, because that which is known about God is evident

within them; for God made it evident to them. For since the creation of the world His invisible attributes, His eternal power and divine nature, have been clearly seen, being understood through what has been made, so that they are without excuse. For even though they knew God, they did not honor Him as God, or give thanks; but they became futile in their speculations, and their foolish heart was darkened. Professing to be wise, they became fools, and exchanged the glory of the incorruptible God for an image in the form of corruptible man and of birds and four-footed animals and crawling creatures."

This judgment happens when people know the truth but reject it. The 1960's generation knew the truth, because it's been around since the first European settlers arrived and built our society upon it. They had more light and truth than practically everyone else in the world, but they rejected both with passion. The Lord's response was to remove His restraining grace, which simply means He lets people go and gives them the sinful freedoms they desire. What that looks like is described in Romans 1:24-32:

"Therefore God gave them over in the lusts of their hearts to impurity, that their bodies might be dishonored among them. For they exchanged the truth of God for a lie, and worshiped and served the creature rather than the Creator, who is blessed forever. Amen. For this reason God gave them over to degrading passions; for their women exchanged the natural function for that which is unnatural, and in the same way also the men abandoned the natural function of the woman and burned in their desire towards one another, men with men committing indecent acts and receiving in their own persons the due penalty of their error. And just as they did not see fit to acknowledge God any longer, God gave them over to a depraved mind, to do those things which are not proper, being filled with all

unrighteousness, wickedness, greed, malice; full of envy, murder, strife, deceit, malice; they are gossips, slanderers, haters of God, insolent, arrogant, boastful, inventors of evil, disobedient to parents, without understanding, untrustworthy, unloving, unmerciful; and although they know the ordinance of God, that those who practice such things are worthy of death, they not only do the same, but also give hearty approval to those who practice them."

That's a truly frightening picture, and it describes *exactly* what has transpired in America from the 1960's through today. Please notice however, that it did not happen all at once. In fact, it happened so gradually that most people weren't aware it was happening at all. The first of God's three-part judgment was to allow a sexual revolution, which inevitably led to the legalization of abortion. His second judgment was to allow a homosexual revolution, which in turn opened the door to every other sexual deviancy. And the third judgment of God was to turn our society over to a depraved mind. This is the most devastating of the three judgments, because when the collective mind of a society is gone, there's very little hope of it ever coming back to sanity. At that point, stage six in the timeline of a nation is almost inevitable. America had reached the depravity stage by the 1990's, and our society has been descending deeper and deeper into madness ever since.

We've just read about a society losing its mind in the book of Romans, but how has this manifested itself in America? Here are a few highlights, which I think paint a fairly accurate picture:

It is when reasoned, logical discussion of any issue becomes almost non-existent and discourse degenerates into a mud-slinging contest, in which the winner is the one who can invent the nastiest insults. When profanity in general and profane expressions involving God or Jesus Christ are commonplace and no longer taboo. When music no longer has a melody, but sounds like the performance of a primitive jungle tribe. When such "music" wins the highest artistic awards. When what we see on the Dr. Phil or the Jerry Springer shows is no longer shocking, but is accepted from coast to coast as normal. When everything that should stay behind closed doors is paraded around in public under the banner of pride. When even after years of parading under this banner, it still hasn't dawned on the proud crowd that pride is the least appealing human characteristic and the most dangerous of all sins. When those with the most deviant and perverted lifestyles are praised and idolized. When lying has become a hugely profitable business, and the greatest liars have proclaimed themselves the final arbiters of all truth. When most TV preachers are con artists. When violent video games, whose graphic scenes of carnage are indistinguishable from the real thing, are considered entertainment. When public schools teach homosexuality, transgenderism, and racist hatred to six-year-old children. When our own government brands parents who object to such teaching *"domestic terrorists."* When many large city neighborhoods are virtual war zones. When some mayors and governors harbor vicious, illegal migrant criminals who terrorize American citizens. When terrorists and pornographers are guaranteed their free speech rights, but doctors are censored. When some drug users serve longer prison sentences than some murderers. When looters and rioters are applauded, and the police take the knee to criminals. When the three strikes law can send a person to prison for life, for stealing a slice of pizza. When law-abiding, tax-paying citizens are sent to prison for years, for defending their homes and families against thieves and murderers. When the burning and vandalizing of churches and synagogues is on the rise, and Jesus is called a racist. When half of all marriages end in divorce, and a quarter of all children are living in one-parent homes. When males are allowed to participate in female sports and to walk away with most of the medals. When privacy in public restrooms is no longer respected and those of the opposite sex are allowed to enter. When many claim they can't define the word "woman." When the mutilation of children has become a hugely profitable business and is applauded by many. When those standing up for God's moral principles are vilified and branded *"hateful, intolerant bigots."* When the least tolerant in our society are continually preaching about tolerance. When the murder of the most innocent is called a *"right."* When Fascists call themselves anti-Fascist (Antifa, whose ideology, tactics, and behavior are identical to Hitler's brown shirts). When the slogan *All Lives Matter* is labeled a racist slogan. When people's lives are routinely destroyed for holding an opinion that someone doesn't like. When most people prefer fairy tales to facts. When those who are hopelessly brainwashed and fast asleep call themselves *"woke."* And finally, when hedonistic narcissists, Communists, Fascists, and criminals are teaching the nation morality. When a society reaches this state, it's abundantly clear that the mental faculties of a significant segment of the population are no longer functioning properly. When such a society still sees itself as *"a shining city on a hill,"* it's absolute proof that it has lost its mind.

God's judgment of abandonment upon a nation is in full effect when there is a complete moral inversion. When that which has always been called evil is called good, and that which has always been called good is called evil. In short, it's when a society has lost all sense of shame and has become an unrestrained demonic madhouse.

While this decades-long demonic party has been going on, the Lord has been sending us a multitude of warnings. By allowing one disaster after another to befall our nation, He's been trying to let us know that unless we cease from our rebellion against Him, the party is coming to an end. And how have we responded to God's warnings? No matter the magnitude of the disaster, the response of the American people is always *exactly the opposite of what the Lord is looking for!* The Lord is looking for humility and shame for offending Him, which should in turn cause us to fall on our knees and to call upon Him for mercy. Furthermore, He is looking for a desire in us to change our wicked ways. But what does He get from us? It's always the same self-serving, arrogant hogwash about how tough, virtuous, and courageous we are, and how we'll rebuild stronger and better. We are Americans after all, and we won't let anything beat us down. Every disaster or crisis has an endless number of "heroes" that are praised to high heaven for some sacrifice, even though most of them are either doing what they're paid to do, or what any decent person would do in the same circumstances.

A perfect example of this type of response, which is so abhorrent to the Lord, came from former U.S. Senator John Edwards, on the third anniversary of the 9/11 attacks. Speaking at the Congressional Black Caucus Prayer Breakfast, this is what John Edwards had to say:

"Good morning. Today, on this day of remembrance and mourning, we have the Lord's word to get us through. 'The bricks

have fallen, but we will build with dressed stones; the sycamores have been cut down, but we will put cedars in their place.' And let me show you how we are building and putting cedars in those three hallowed places – the footprints of the Towers, the Pentagon, and the field in Pennsylvania. Walk with me through this day and you will see that this is a season of hope. In America, we always rise up. Sometimes not on the first day or the second day, but we begin to rise up and build something new. This is who we are, and this is the eternal spirit of America."

Besides the arrogance which the Lord hates, there's something else wrong with these remarks. The meaning of the Bible verses John Edwards quoted is exactly the opposite of the way he used them. Those verses refer to a disaster which the Lord allowed to befall Israel, and instead of humbling themselves and repenting, the children of Israel became even more arrogant and boastful. To get a clearer understanding of these verses in context, here's the entire passage from the book of Isaiah 9:8-12: *"The Lord sends a message against Jacob, And it falls on Israel. And all the people know it, That is, Ephraim and the inhabitants of Samaria, Asserting in pride and in arrogance of heart; 'the bricks have fallen down, But we will rebuild with smooth stones; The Sycamores have been cut down, But we will replace them with cedars.' Therefore the Lord raises against them adversaries from Rezin, And spurs their enemies on, The Syrians on the east and the Philistines on the west; And they devour Israel with gaping jaws."* The Lord brought punishment on the children of Israel for responding to disaster the way John Edwards responded. The next time the Lord tries to get our attention through some disaster, it might be a good idea for us to hear what He's saying, instead of tickling each other's ears with arrogant, narcissistic delusions about how great we are. *Every one of His warning judgments has been a one-word message to America, and that message is: REPENT!*

The discussion of the depravity stage of America wouldn't be complete without taking a brief look at America's Holocaust, *the murder of more than 60 million babies in about 50 years!* As stated earlier, killing the most innocent is now considered a "right," and a Constitutional one at that. That's quite a claim, but is the murder of the unborn *really* a Constitutional right? The pro-choice side has had since 1973 to show us where exactly such a right can be found in our Constitution, but they've been strangely silent. Do you suppose they've not enlightened us, because no such Constitutional right actually exists? I believe we can be absolutely certain of that. However, even *if* such a right could be found in our Constitution, it wouldn't amount to a hill of beans. The fact of the matter is that the Lord has made Himself abundantly clear about what *He* thinks about the shedding of innocent blood. *He calls it an abomination, and His Word carries a lot more weight than any law, or even the word of all Americans combined!*

If the pro-choice side could present a well reasoned argument that their position is a moral one, those on the other side might listen. But the only thing we've heard from them for 50 years is slogans. *"It's my body," "Pro-choice," "A woman's right to choose," "Exercising my reproductive rights."*

Choice is a wonderful thing, because without it we'd be robots or slaves, but is *anyone* pro-choice about *everything*? We can be pro-choice about many things, but every sane person would agree that some choices are not ours to make. No one would deny that the slogan is cute and appealing, but it carries no moral weight in regard to this issue. The same applies to the one about exercising one's reproductive rights. It sounds legitimate, but what does *murder* have to do with reproductive rights? Finally, no one in the pro-life movement cares anything about what a woman does with *her* body. The *only* body any of us care anything about is the body of a baby about to be killed.

A hundred years ago, there may have been some excuse for thinking that a fetus is just a piece of lifeless tissue. Sonograms didn't exist in those days, but now we can all see the baby in the womb, moving its fingers and toes, and even smiling. It doesn't look like lifeless tissue, or like some unrecognizable creature. It looks just like a human baby.

The pro-choice side doesn't like to debate the issue, because they can't win a debate. They can't defend their position, because their position is indefensible. They therefore resort to the only methods available to sway public opinion. Slogans, media bias, censorship of free speech, and personal attacks against anyone who speaks the truth.

The next time you meet those who support legalized abortion, you might wish to ask them the following question: *Are you glad your mother didn't abort you, or do you wish she did?* They'll probably scream and holler that it's a trick question, but it's actually not. Just about all of them are extremely happy that they're alive, and that they were granted the opportunity to experience the marvels of God's creation. The question is designed to get them to think past the slogans, and to ask themselves why they're so fanatically passionate about denying the gift of life to others.

We have known for decades that a baby in the womb feels pain. Try to imagine the pain involved in having your limbs torn from your body. Is this not reason enough for *everyone* to oppose the practice of abortion?

If you wish to know just how barbaric most modern abortions are, I recommend a six-minute video of a former abortion practitioner, Dr. Anthony Levatino, testifying before a Congressional Committee. Dr. Levatino has performed over 1,200 abortions, so he's an expert on the subject. You can find the video on YouTube, if they haven't yet removed it for *"spreading medical misinformation."* The name of it is *Ex-abortion doctor tells the shocking truth about abortion.* I challenge all who support this practice to watch it, and *not* change their mind about this issue.

We all know about God's prohibition of murder, and the discovery of DNA leaves no doubt about how this prohibition is related to abortion. *Different DNA, different person!* Murder is murder, no matter how small the human being, or where that human being happens to reside. End of discussion, case closed.

Every sin has within it its own punishment. This can be clearly seen with sexual promiscuity and with homosexuality. The first leads to a host of sexually transmitted diseases, shame, guilt, and broken relationships. The second has the added punishment of a drastically shortened lifespan. On average, homosexuals live about twenty years shorter lives than heterosexuals. When it comes to abortion, the punishment is the usual shame and guilt, sometimes even leading to suicide. On a national scale, the punishment is even greater. We all know that Social Security and Medicare are going bankrupt, but someone crunched some numbers and discovered that both programs would be solvent for decades to come, if there were about *60 million* additional taxpayers. Where have we heard that number before? The best way to sum this up is with a verse from the book of Galatians 6:7: *"Do not be deceived, God is not mocked; for whatever a man sows, this he will also reap."*

When Satan offers people sinful freedoms, he never attaches disclaimers that warn us about the dangers of those sinful freedoms. He never tells us that if partake, we might destroy our lives, or die years before our time. He sells his merchandise in lovely packages, and people usually don't find out it's poison until it's too late. When we look back at the last sixty years in America, it's amazing to see how much poison he's been able to sell to the American people. What's even more amazing is that they still keep buying it.

The Lord is incredibly patient, but there does come a point when His patience finally runs out. It seems that in 2020, God's patience with America ran out, and we entered the sixth stage of our nation's history. A massive amount of destruction has come upon our nation since 2020. Our society is collapsing before our eyes and seems to be descending into a bottomless pit. Is there any way to stop the descent and reverse course? Theoretically yes, but practically no.

One of the problems is the fact that some very powerful people have a vested interest in seeing America come to utter ruin, so that it can be easily integrated into a one-world government. In addition to this, way too many Americans still don't have a clue about what is happening and continue to buy into the lies.

If our nation is to have any hope of recovery, the change must begin in the heart. The first thing we must do is be honest about the spiritual condition of our nation, as well as our own. The fact of the matter is that no nation in the history of the world has ever gone as far in rebelling against God as America, and has ever come back to tell us about it. The Lord's warning judgments are now descending on our nation in rapid succession, and from all indications, most people don't seem to have any desire to mend their ways and get right with the Lord. Way too many are still shaking their fists at Him and spitting in His face.

We can expect to see more and more warning judgments with the Lord's one-word message. Some places will receive more than others, and we should pay special attention to California. It leads the nation in evil, and unless it ceases its rebellion, it will continue to receive the brunt of God's judgments. May what happens to California in the time remaining serve as a warning to the rest of the nation.

If this book should reach the Hollywood crowd, and they begin to howl with laughter, please don't take them too seriously. Mockers do have their day, but when they mock and laugh, picture in your mind's eye Noah building a giant ship, as all his his neighbors were howling with laughter. Then picture the first drops of rain, and the surprised look in their eyes. Picture them still laughing, but less and less so as the water started to rise. And finally, picture the terror on their faces and the absence of laughter when the water reached their chins! I'm certain that most of the Hollywood crowd and a multitude of ordinary Americans, will continue to laugh and mock the Lord until the final day. The California mockers in particular should take note of the fact that they are living on major fault lines, and that the Lord has mercifully delayed the coming of "the big one." When His patience with California does finally run out and He removes His hand of protection, just as with Noah's neighbors, water will be the judgment. History keeps repeating itself, and it's been said that the most important thing we can learn from history, is that most people never learn anything from history.

It has been understood and accepted by globalists for well over 200 years that when their one-world government comes into being, it will be run from Washington. In this however, they are greatly mistaken. There's some disagreement among Bible scholars about where it will be run from, but almost everyone agrees that it *won't* be Washington. The great irony in this is that American globalists and those who've participated in their crimes, have destroyed their own country for *absolutely nothing!* They are like the guests that arrive at a sumptuous dinner for cannibals, wondering who's for dinner. Then they hear the doors lock, and realize much too late, *it's them!*

The Scripture verse that highlights America's greatest sin and foreshadows catastrophic days ahead for our nation is Proverbs 16:18: *"Pride goes before destruction, And a haughty spirit before stumbling."* The Word of God issues many warnings to the proud, who think that turning morality on its head is a mark of superior intelligence and sophistication. Here's one of those warnings: *"Woe to those who call evil good, and good evil; Who substitute darkness for light and light for darkness; Who substitute bitter for sweet, and sweet for bitter! Woe to those who are wise in their own eyes, and clever in their own sight!"* Isaiah 5:20-21. Those who mock God and think that His warnings to us are one big joke, would do well to remember one very important thing. *The Lord always has the last word, and the last laugh.*

THE FIFTH COLUMN

People believe there's a great struggle between Communism and Capitalism. It will therefore come as a shock when I say that there's no struggle between Communism and Capitalism at all. At least not in the way people think. It's true that Communism and Capitalism are polar opposites, and in that sense, they *are* at war for the minds and hearts of people. But what most people have never grasped and understood is that *from the very beginning, Communism has simply been a tool of the Capitalist globalists.*

It is an established historical fact that the Communist Revolution in Russia in 1917, was financed by western Capitalists. Since Communism is not an economically viable system, western Capitalists subsidized Russia until Communism's *supposed* fall in 1989. I say supposed, because only a cursory examination of the facts show very clearly that in Russia itself, no fundamental change ever took place. An Oligarchy was created in Russia, which is essentially being run by Communists. The people who were in power *before* "the fall of Communism," are the same people who are in power now. If a real regime change had taken place in Russia, Vladimir Putin, the former Head of the KGB, would most certainly not hold the position he does. He would either have been one of the first executed, or he'd now be rotting in prison. But instead, good old Vlad has been nonchalantly running Russia for years.

The reason I brought this up was to illustrate that in the world of politics, all is smoke and mirrors and nothing is as it seems. It's obvious that in the geopolitical chess game the globalists are playing, creating the illusion that Russian Communism is no longer a threat to America was very important to them. It's just as important to them to create the illusion that Capitalism in America is being dismantled. There's no question that many Americans are beginning to embrace Communism and are applauding the destruction of Capitalism, but those who love our country need to know what is *really* going on. What we are witnessing is the destruction of Capitalism for the people, so that it would belong exclusively to the globalists.

There are two versions of Communism. The one that is sold to the gullible, and the one the unfortunate suckers have to live with when they finally get it. The fairy tale version promises a utopia where everything is free, and we all live happily ever after. The real version is a nightmare beyond imagination. Anyone who has ever lived under such a system would heartily attest to that. Unfortunately, many Americans can't wait for the nightmare to arrive on our doorstep. A huge number are actively fighting for it.

The Capitalist globalists are fighting for it harder than anyone. They are spending vast amounts of money to support leftist causes and Communist organizations like *Black Lives Matter,* which seems like a very strange thing for Capitalists to do. But it makes perfect sense, because turning the country into a Communist police state will make it much easier for them to control people and rob them even more. Their Covid lockdowns were essentially a trial run for Communism in America and the rest of the world, but they had another important function. Since 2020, the globalists have succeeded in driving a significant percentage of small businesses into bankruptcy, and their mega corporations have been filling the vacuum. Isn't it strange that many small businesses were deemed non-essential during the lockdowns and had to close their doors, while all the globalist businesses which sold the same products and services were deemed essential and were allowed to stay open? It's all been quite ingenious and diabolical.

Every time the globalists create some crisis or run some scam, they always end up with more and everyone else ends up with less. It's a very sophisticated way of robbing people, and no matter how obvious their crimes, they're never held accountable. The reason this is so, is because there exists an unwritten rule that the wealthiest in this world can do virtually anything they like with no legal consequences. The globalists aren't subjects of any jurisdiction and can't be summoned before any court. They don't answer to *any* government, *all* governments answer to them.

Americans started out as free people, but they've gradually been transformed into obedient slaves, who continually allow themselves to be scammed. We'll look at only a few highlights of that transformation. The first major step was the introduction of compulsory education. It seemed innocent at the time, because people believe that education is positive. But it gave the social engineers a tremendous tool to mold children into the kind of citizens the government wanted. That can be good or bad, depending on what kind of government we have. Many believe that if something is positive, making it compulsory must be a societal improvement. The fallacy of this kind of thinking can be easily refuted. Suppose I invited you for a nice steak dinner, and you came, enjoyed it, and it didn't cost you a dime. That would be a great thing. But what if I forced you at the point of a gun to have a free steak dinner with me every night of the week? Do you think you would enjoy that steak as much? A hundred years ago, compulsory public education in America may have at least *resembled* a delicious steak dinner, but today's fare doesn't even resemble junk food and it's pure poison. Many of today's educators are doing horrendous damage to impressionable children in the compulsory public schools. They are warping their minds in countless ways, in an effort to transform as many as possible into reprobates like themselves. Just one example of this warping of the mind is the teaching of the revisionist history of Critical Race Theory. It has confused an entire generation of Americans and helped groom the rioters of 2020. Instead of teaching the *facts* of history, many schools are teaching a delusional, hateful *theory*, which is now tearing our society to shreds.

Another step toward turning America into a Communist police state was the introduction of the *"war on drugs"* in the late 1800's. This may be the most destructive social policy our government ever invented. It was first used against Native Americans to keep them docile and to prevent further rebellion. Later, it was used against Chinese immigrants, who were despised by many Americans due to their strange culture and customs. One unique feature of their culture was a fondness for opium, and this made them easy targets.

In the 1920's, the war on drugs took a temporary backseat to Prohibition, which was another social experiment that had devastating results. Prohibition came into being through the lobbying efforts of the *Women's Temperance League,* whose members felt that it was their obligation to dictate their own personal morality to the nation. They believed that too many men were getting too drunk and neglecting their families. The rent wasn't getting paid and the baby wasn't getting milk, so their brilliant idea was to make alcohol illegal. Once Prohibition got going, the rent still wasn't getting paid and the baby still wasn't getting milk, but the added bonus was that people were drinking *twice as much as before!* There were other added bonuses that the geniuses didn't envision. One of them was the explosion of crime, mostly through violent gangs. Whenever a product is made illegal, there is an instant demand for that product, and criminals are more than happy to supply that demand. Does that sound strangely familiar? But the crime wasn't just limited to gangs. Massive corruption infiltrated law enforcement and the judicial system. There was so much easy money floating around that everyone wanted a piece of the pie. Practically everyone was drinking, and practically everyone was on the take. That should definitely sound familiar. At the end of seven years of this societal nightmare, those that lobbied for it begged Congress to repeal Prohibition. When Congress finally repealed it, crime went down at once, and alcohol consumption gradually returned to normal.

You'd think the American public would learn something from this, but as I said earlier, people don't learn from history. They keep making the same mistakes over and over, until they finally manage to destroy their society. In the 1960's, the war on drugs went into high gear. The people turned their backs on God, which of course emboldened the tyrants. They began jailing people and building more prisons. The devastation that this social policy brought upon

America and the world cannot be calculated. Many otherwise law-abiding, productive citizens are now serving years-long prison sentences for recreational drug use! Inasmuch as a quarter of all children are raised in one-parent families, over the years, millions of children have been made wards of the state! Instead of contributing to the National Treasury, hundreds of thousands of Americans are being housed in prisons, at a minimum cost of $30,000 a year per inmate! Through the introduction of asset forfeiture laws, the government has been able to confiscate people's cars, boats, houses, farms, and businesses! Gang turf wars have devastated many cities, as criminals fight among each other over the drug trade! Police and judges are on the take, as in the days of Prohibition! All black-market products become extremely expensive, which leads to more crime! The most powerful drug lords have become billionaires! Central America and parts of South America have become politically destabilized and have turned into war zones, because drug cartels are better armed and more powerful than some governments! People are taught to snitch on their neighbors! Families are torn apart for years, as loved ones are shipped off to prisons! The list goes on and on, and you can probably think of a few gems yourself. Would you like to know why many Americans, including some misguided Christians, think all this is good for our society? It's simple. *Because it's been going on for as long as we've been alive, and because our government and the people on television say so!*

Some people might say that all this is necessary, because drugs are bad for you. I tend to agree that drugs are bad for you, but I wonder if those same people have ever considered that there are an endless number of things in this world that are bad for you. Can you imagine locking up everyone who does anything that was bad for them? *Who would be left to guard the prisoners?* Cyanide and arsenic are also bad for you, but can you imagine someone taking a lick and getting sick, and after that being sent to prison for 20 years?

Schizophrenia is a mental condition in which a person can hold completely opposing views at the same time without blinking an eye. We've already talked about abortion proponents, who base their entire argument on the slogan *it's my body.* As we've seen, that argument is fallacious, because it's not *their* body that's at issue. But since that argument seems to convince so many, why don't they apply it to drugs? The same government that encourages and subsidizes abortion is also sending people to prison, because of what they do with *their body!* That resembles national schizophrenia!

Illegal drugs are responsible for about 30,000 deaths a year in America. The globalist pharmaceutical companies push *legal* drugs, which are responsible for at least 100,000 deaths a year in America. Our society is destroying itself over the first death toll, and pretends like the second death toll doesn't even exist. Please notice that whenever and wherever the globalists make an appearance, there's always mass death and destruction. Please also notice that in the case of illegal drugs, the *users* go to prison, but in the case of legal drugs that have killed people, the *pushers* remain free and are allowed to get even richer.

As a side note, there's the issue of staggering national hypocrisy. Please consider the fact that America is the most drug-addicted nation on the face of the earth. Yet, we have the audacity to dictate drug policy to the entire world. There are places where people have been smoking opium or hashish for hundreds of years, without it causing any major societal problems. But here's Johnny come lately America that can't even clean up its own backyard, but we think we have the right to tell everyone on the planet what to do. Many Americans wonder why the world hates us so much. I would humbly suggest that our national arrogance is the number one reason.

Much more can be said about the hidden motives behind this destructive social policy, but based only on what we can see with our own eyes, the "war on drugs" more closely resembles a "war on people." Inasmuch as it has destroyed tens of millions of lives, does anyone still believe it has anything to do with saving lives?

In what other ways have many Americans been unknowingly indoctrinated into Communist ideology, and have thereby become the fifth column? The list is endless, and we'll look at a couple, but first let me explain what a fifth column is. The term is attributed to Spanish General Emilio Mola Vidal. During the Spanish Civil War, the General's troops surrounded Madrid in four columns, east, west, north, and south. Someone remarked to the General that he should be able to take the city easily with those four columns. The General replied that the four columns were good, but that the one he's counting on to take the city is the fifth column. The one that was in the city itself! While we are continually preoccupied with Communist threats outside our borders, we seem to have completely forgotten about the fifth column that's inside them!

It's not too difficult to recognize that organizations like *Antifa* and *Black Lives Matter* are a part of the fifth column. They openly state it. It's also clear that most college and university professors are a part of it. They openly embrace Marxist ideology and successfully indoctrinate many of their students. Some in the mainstream media are a part of it, because they also embrace Marxist ideology and ceaselessly try to indoctrinate the entire nation. Many government officials who enact and enforce oppressive Communistic laws are also a part of it. Finally, it's not an exaggeration to say that everyone in America has friends, neighbors, or family members, who have been deceived and have become a part of the fifth column.

Many years ago, Communists coined a term to describe those living in free societies, who are knowingly or unknowingly helping them in the destruction of their own societies, so that a Communist police state can emerge. The term they came up with was *useful idiots*. It's particularly well-suited to those who are *knowingly* working to establish such a regime in America. One of the reasons it may be too late to save America, is because today the fifth column of useful idiots in our nation is a giant army.

Over the years, most Americans seem to have been sleeping or didn't care, as our government passed one oppressive and unjust law after another. Some have been deceived into believing that a law is right because it's a law, but I would suggest that something is right because it's right, not because it's a law. Many prisons around the world are packed to the rafters with innocent people who broke some law. So, how many of our laws are unjust? Judging only by the ones we know about, it's probably more than any of us can count.

One law that is clearly unjust is the seat belt law. Some people think it's no big deal, that it's just a petty nuisance. But it's much more than that, because tyrants use petty nuisances as stepping-stones to greater injustices. When this abomination was first introduced, the vast majority of the public were opposed to it. That alone should have ended it on the spot. From cradle to grave, we're being fed the same old lines about "the will of the people" and a "representative government," but it's been evident for decades that we have barely any say at all.

Because it's essentially a money-making scam, the tyrants and the insurance companies wanted this law in the worst way, so naturally it was shoved down our throats. Failing to wear a seat belt causes no one else harm, but if we don't wear one, our government says we've committed a crime. But who have we committed this crime against? The answer is obvious. Against the tyrants whose order we didn't obey. The public has been told through mind-numbing propaganda that this law is for our protection, because the government cares about our well-being. But what if we don't want this particular type of protection? It doesn't matter, we get it whether we want it or not, and if we refuse to comply, the tyrants will cheerfully slap us with a $200 fine, just to show how much they care. If we violate this Communistic law a few times, we may even lose our license to drive. What amazes me are ordinary Americans who argue in support of the seat belt law. Some of them are so passionate, it's as though they think that repealing it would mean they'd be *forbidden* to wear one.

Another one of those stepping-stone laws was the mandating of non-smoking sections in restaurants. When first hearing about it, I suspected that it was the beginning of something more sinister. Non-smokers loved it, and smokers didn't care, because they could still smoke in the smoking section. But something seemed strange to me. Whenever the issue was mentioned, more often than not, it was also stated that a restaurant is a *public* place. This was clearly a deception, because while it *is* true that the public congregates in restaurants, this does not make them public places. A restaurant is no more a public place than your backyard when a bunch of your friends show up for a cookout. From a legal standpoint, it's a *private business enterprise.* An example of a public place would be the county courthouse. It was clear that there was some agenda in play, and it became even clearer when shortly thereafter, all restaurants were mandated to be completely smoke-free. The lying media clouded the issue by incessantly talking about health, but this was just a diversionary tactic to steer people away from the real issue. The fact of the matter is that this is a *private property issue.* If business owners don't have the right to do or not to do business with anyone they choose, then the words "private property" have no meaning at all. These restaurant smoking bans set a very dangerous precedent, which as we all know is currently being used to force business owners to violate their conscience. Imbedded in these Communistic bans is also an unspoken but unmistakable message to all Americans that *the government can arbitrarily decide what is, and what isn't private property.* Today, the tyrants' redefining of private and public applies to restaurants, but tomorrow they may change those definitions yet again and apply them to your house.

It was inevitable that bars would eventually become the next target. Many businesses were run into bankruptcy just this way. Anti-smoking fanatics have never understood this issue, and most of them probably never will. The reason for this is that for most Americans, every issue is always all about me. If it suits me, it's good, if it doesn't, it's bad. No thought ever seems to be given to how a particular issue affects anyone else, or our society at large. Those who applaud these bans seriously believe that their personal preference is more important than someone's right to run their business as they see fit, or even to earn a living. If someone doesn't like something about a particular business, passing laws which run that business into bankruptcy is not the solution. A much simpler solution is to not frequent that business. That's the meaning of free enterprise.

To illustrate what these bans are *really* about, I'll share a local TV news story. It's about a bar owner and one solitary customer in his establishment. Both were smokers, and when they wanted to light up, they went outside. It happened to be a very frigid winter day, and both men were shivering in front of a warm and empty bar. The entire scene was pathetic and humiliating, and then it hit me. Humiliating people and showing them who's boss are the real reasons for this charade. It may interest people to know that smoking bans were a prominent feature of Nazi Germany. When constructing a dictatorship, every little precedent for government overreach is immensely useful to tyrants, because once that dictatorship is fully constructed, people will think it's just business as usual. Without even realizing it, they've been gradually conditioned to accept tyranny as a completely normal state of affairs.

The pretense about the bans having anything to do with health went out the window when they included public parks and rest areas. It would be an outrage if someone caught a whiff of cigarette smoke in a park or a rest area, but it's perfectly acceptable for the factory down the street to fill the countryside with noxious fumes for miles around. But even this wasn't enough, because for tyrants, no amount of tyranny is ever enough. So, the next phase of their operation started forbidding smoking in private cars when children were inside. Can anyone guess what might be next? I'd better not say it, because it might give the tyrants ideas. On second thought, I'm sure they've already thought of it, and are probably working on it as we speak.

Today's America is nothing like most people imagine it to be. The problem issues I've shed light on are just the tip of the iceberg. In principle, we still have the Bill of Rights, but in reality, most of them are hanging by a thread. Furthermore, the left/right paradigm of the two major political parties is a masterful illusion. To illustrate the real political paradigm in today's America, think of your dining room table as the entire political spectrum. Place two toothpicks side by side on the left side of the table. The left edge of the table is a Communist police state, and the two toothpicks represent the Democrat and Republican Parties. The one closest to the edge of the table is the Democrat Party, and the one to the right of it is the Republican Party. The right side of the table is where America began in 1776. The whole political establishment has been moving toward the left for decades. Anyone who doubts this should consider the fact that the average Democrat when JFK was President was more conservative than the average Republican today. Many freedom lovers believe that the Republican Party will save us, but they are sadly mistaken. While the party of Abraham Lincoln still holds the moral high ground on certain cultural issues, today it's just as corrupt as the party of woke delusions and serves primarily the interests of the globalists. The entire political establishment in America is like a runaway train speeding toward a leftist societal disaster. The Democrat Party may be the engine car driving the train, but the Republican Party is the caboose.

The sad truth is that *both* parties have been robbing the American people of their civil liberties for a very long time. Both have granted the government the legal authority to listen to phone conversations, to read e-mails, and to spy on citizens in a hundred different ways. They've also granted the government the authority to search anything and anyone for virtually any reason, to arrest anyone for virtually any reason, and to confiscate private property indiscriminately, and sometimes without due process. The acts of brutal government tyranny endorsed by both parties cannot be counted, but to give you a tiny glimpse into the type of activities our government has been engaged in for decades, here's just one: SWAT teams were dispatched in some places to arrest extremely dangerous American farmers for committing the horrendous crime of selling unpasteurized milk to their neighbors!

Per capita, America incarcerates more people than any nation on earth. Over the years, *millions* have been incarcerated for absolutely nothing! But don't worry, our leaders haven't been abusing the American people just on a whim. They first made sure to pass some laws, so the tyranny would be proper and legal.

This is the *real* America, but many Americans are still living in the America of the Lee Greenwood song, in which he tells us that he's proud to be an American, because at least here he knows he's free. Melody wise it's a fairly decent song, but the words are totally inappropriate for today, because the America he's singing about is long gone. We're still not where China is, but that's the direction we're headed, and at the rate we're moving, it won't be very long before we're there. *Public servants* is the title we've chosen for our elected representatives and all other public officials, but based upon many of their actions for the last few decades, wouldn't a better description for most of them be *tyrants*?

One wonders how much tyranny needs to be imposed before it finally begins to dawn on people that they're no longer free. Through massive mind control and social engineering, a frightening number of flag-waving Americans have been turned into Communists without even knowing it. If you told these people that this is essentially what they are, they'd be insulted. But they think like Communists, defend tyranny like Communists, and march in single file like Communists. Every snippet of independent thought has been systematically beaten out of them. These Americans would find the world of the founding fathers uncomfortable and somewhat terrifying, *because of an abundance of freedom!* They'd have a difficult time understanding how a society could even function, without the government controlling everything.

So, what's at the root of this astounding transformation of our society? How can people who have been taught to hate the word *"Communism,"* have ever come to love the ideology that it represents? There are two very important ways this has been achieved. The first, is that they have never been taught the foundational principles of freedom, and the second is by the clever substitution of other words for the word *"Communism."* But where can the foundational principles of freedom be found? Since our society doesn't seem to have them anymore, have they been locked away in some vault, or hidden in some cave? Not at all. They can be found in the same place every other foundational principle of life can be found. In the book that has been banned in America's public schools, the one our society was founded upon, and the one that is gathering dust in most American homes. *The Holy Bible.*

A DIRE WARNING
TO LOST REBELS

Not all lies are the same. Some are just a silly nuisance. Some can cost us a few bucks. Some can break our hearts. Some can destroy our families. Some can destroy an entire society. Some can kill us. *And some can take us straight to hell!*

If two people are trying to convince us of diametrically opposed things, and both present an equally powerful argument, which one are we to believe? If we knew nothing about either of them, it would be a toss up. To have a better chance of knowing which one is telling us the truth, it would be helpful to find out something about the character of both, and it would be especially helpful to know whether either party has ever lied before. From the beginning, the Lord and Satan have been telling mankind a completely different story. Each one has called the other a liar, so which one of them is telling us the truth?

In the Garden of Eden, the Lord told Adam and Eve not to eat the fruit of a particular tree, and He warned them that if they did, they would die. Satan came along and told Eve to eat the fruit, and assured her that she would most definitely *not* die. Adam and Eve ate the fruit and died, so we can chalk up one lie for Satan. Since that day, the Lord and Satan have established an unbroken record. The Lord has an unbroken record of telling people the truth, and Satan has an unbroken record of telling people lies. Based on this, we might conclude that most people would choose to believe the Lord, but that has never been the case. From the Garden until this very day, most people have believed Satan.

The reason most people overlook Satan's history of deception and choose to believe him anyway, is because he peddles the same appealing temptations that led to the fall. *Self-will, pride, and the promise to become just like God.* His whole kingdom is appealing, because he tells people exactly what they want to hear, and the only rule in it is *do what thou wilt.* In contrast, the Lord doesn't tell us what we want to hear, but what we *need* to hear, and to most people, this is not appealing at all.

God's kingdom and Satan's kingdom are as different from each other as can be, but because the devil always tries to mimic the Lord, the differences aren't always immediately obvious. Both kingdoms claim the moral high ground, but one is infinitely righteous, while the other is infinitely wicked. Jesus told us how we can distinguish one from the other in Matthew 7:18: *"A good tree cannot produce bad fruit, nor can a rotten tree produce good fruit."*

It all comes down to God's moral Law, which is embodied in the Ten Commandments. It shows us how righteous God is and how unrighteous we are. Jesus explained that we can violate God's moral Law even by our thoughts. This of course makes the gap between God's righteousness and our wickedness even greater. The entirety of God's moral Law can be summed up by two basic commands. We are to love the Lord supremely with all our faculties, and we are to love our neighbor as we love ourselves.

We all fail miserably on both counts, which leaves absolutely no room for pride, but that's the very thing Satan tempts us with. So, we're left with a choice. Either God's moral Law or pride has to go.

Once a society abandons God's moral Law, a vacuum is created. But since every society needs some order, the boldest begin to play God. The first perverted thought to enter their minds is that *everyone ought to think and live like me.* That's a sick way of looking at the world, but no harm is done if it stops there. The problem is that many take it to the next level and think *there ought to be a law to make everyone think and live like me.* This is where most societal problems and conflicts begin, as was the case with Prohibition. In fairness, it must be admitted that even some Christians were led astray in that particular fiasco. Prohibition was a graphic illustration of what happens when self-righteous moralizers try to impose their own *personal* morality on others.

God's Word gives us very important guidelines about what should and what should not be legislated by earthly governments. But those who turn their backs on God and His Word legislate whatever their sinful minds can conceive. The 1960's generation is an example of this. Initially, they condemned the establishment, but the moment they *became* the establishment, they began to legislate every imaginable abomination. It didn't take them long to abandon their motto *live and let live,* and to substitute it with the motto *live and tell everyone how to live.* Hypocrisy truly knows no bounds. Trying to impose our will on others is perhaps the clearest evidence of our sinful and depraved human nature. God has given us His moral Law and reason, which tell us where we end and where other people begin. For those who need a little help, I would suggest that *we end at the tips of our noses.*

Those who love the Lord and their neighbor have no choice but to live and let live. Many unjust, Communistic laws would be immediately repealed, if our elected representatives had the slightest respect for God, His Word, and their fellow man. The principle of live and let live runs throughout the Bible, and it is best summarized in Proverbs 3:29-30. *"Do not devise harm against your neighbor, While he lives in security beside you. Do not contend with a man without cause, If he has done you no harm."*

It has been said that the apple doesn't fall far from the tree, so it's no surprise that the children of the 1960's generation became even greater self-righteous moralizers and tyrants than their parents. The grandchildren have taken this Communist ideology to the final stage, and we saw them destroying their neighbors' property and burning American cities. They demonstrated extreme hate for their neighbor, but by some mental sleight of hand they've convinced themselves that they are moral and that those who refuse to join them in their criminal enterprise are not. It would have been way too tedious and time-consuming to coerce everyone through the legislative process, as their grandparents and parents did. So instead, they decided to speed things up with torches and bricks, and the globalists who brainwashed them are beside themselves with joy. In the streets, the halls of Congress, and everywhere in between, the globalists found more than enough useful idiots, who are happy to do their dirty work for them and to hand them the country. From the 1960's to today, this has been the fruit of a thoroughly rotten tree, and this is what politics in Satan's kingdom looks like.

Spirituality in Satan's kingdom is a sight to behold as well. The father of lies is a master counterfeiter, and his specialty is counterfeit Christianity. Most seminaries are filling the pulpits of America with deceived deceivers, who are filling the pews with false converts. The Prince of Darkness does his best work in churches on Sunday morning, rather than nightclubs the night before. He desires honor and a following, and he can get both much easier through false teachers with a Bible than with drunks.

About 70% of the American people profess to be Christians, and almost everyone believes the dominant religion in America is Christianity. I believe that is demonstrably false. Today, the dominant religion in America is *paganism that masquerades as Christianity.* Some may find that statement shocking, but I wish to present just two pieces of evidence that show this is in fact the case. Approximately 60% of adult Americans support legalized abortion. The Lord could not have been any clearer on this issue, so if 70% of Americans are Christians, the maximum amount of support legalized abortion could possibly have is 30%. The Lord is just as clear in His Word about the issue of homosexuality. He calls it an abomination, and there shouldn't be any confusion about what that means. But same-sex marriage now has the support of perhaps 70% of the American public. So, what exactly is the problem? Don't people know what the Lord has said about these issues? Yes, people know full well what the Lord has said about these, and many other issues. *They simply don't care.* They believe that their own opinions carry much more weight than God's Word. This is a horror, but what's even worse is that many of these people have the audacity to call themselves Christians.

When it comes to foundational doctrines of the Christian faith, many professing Christians display the same contempt for what the Word of God teaches. They call themselves believers, but what do they actually believe? The answer is that they believe whatever they want to believe. If God's Word contradicts their beliefs in any way, they simply find a church that affirms them. With more than 400 English translations of the Bible in circulation and deceivers in most pulpits, it's easy for everyone to create their own version of Christianity. What these people never seem to ask themselves however, is whether it's possible to despise certain portions of God's Word and at the same time love God.

The majority of people prefer paganism over Christianity, because it gives them much more freedom to live their lives as they please. But saying *I'm a pagan* doesn't have as nice a ring to it as saying *I'm a Christian*. So, Satan came up with a perfect way for people to remain pagans, but be able to identify as Christians. *The modern presentation of the Gospel.* It's been around for at least a century, and we've all heard it. *Admit that you're a sinner and accept Jesus into your heart, because he has a wonderful plan for your life.* If you do this, you're told that you are now a child of God. Unfortunately, this is not a presentation of the Gospel. First of all, even the worst sinner can admit he's not perfect, so there's nothing noble about admitting the obvious. Secondly, since most people have accepted a lot of creepy people into their hearts, why not accept Jesus as well? So, there's nothing particularly noble about this either. Thirdly, the main things Jesus promised his disciples in this life are trials, afflictions, and persecution.

This unbiblical Gospel presentation accounts for most "Christian conversions" in America for the last hundred years. Catholics are told that if they partake of few sacraments throughout their lives, and do enough good works, they *might* make it to heaven. But since they can't know how many good works are enough, there's no way they can ever have any assurance of salvation. By not knowing what God's Word says very clearly about salvation, most people are totally confused about the issue. What people *should* know is that while the Lord has made salvation *available* to all, entering His kingdom is *not* easy. There *are* conditions and there *is* a cost.

Most mainline denominations not only fail to preach the Gospel, but they deny many foundational doctrines of the Christian faith. As far as they're concerned, it doesn't matter what anyone believes, which makes me wonder why they even bother to hold church services. Could it be because church has become just another business? They seem to spend more of their time pushing government propaganda than teaching God's Word, and the worst of them shamelessly celebrate what the Lord calls abominations. They're not attempting to change the culture, they *are* the culture. To compound the problem further, most TV preachers are charlatans who twist the Scriptures for money, and some "Christian" television networks feature an almost 24/7 parade of these heretics. That doesn't mean that faithful preachers can't be found on television, but they're vastly outnumbered by the deceivers. To compound the problem even further, many "Christian" music artists are putting out very strange messages in their music, and some of their album covers are filled with Satanic and witchcraft symbols. To sum it all up, instead of leading the nation toward God's light, most churches are leading it deeper and deeper into an abyss of darkness. The message from most pulpits is *do what thou wilt!*

Many have taken that message to heart and are doing just that. They abuse their spouses and children, but it's okay, because they've accepted Jesus into their hearts. They treat relatives, friends, neighbors, and strangers like dirt, but that's okay too, because Jesus is in their hearts while they're doing so. They lie, cheat, and steal, and that of course is okay as well, because Jesus forgave them for all that when they accepted Him into their hearts. Hating, cursing, blaspheming, and engaging in every kind of abominable behavior is perfectly okay for many people, because they can even remember the day and hour that they accepted Jesus into their hearts. What these people are giving testimony to however, is that *Jesus is not, and never has been in their hearts.* What I've just said may be misinterpreted as promoting some type of works salvation, but that's not the case at all. What's makes the people I mentioned different from genuine believers is that their godless behavior and attitudes are *always* accompanied by no sense of shame and no desire to change. They're fully convinced that they're not doing anything wrong, so why should they wish to change? All of this is the fruit of a thoroughly rotten tree, and this is what spirituality in Satan's kingdom looks like.

Those who expose the shocking hypocrisy of what is passing itself off as Christianity in today's America, are continually being attacked and called judgmental. I've been attacked myself, simply for telling people what the Lord has to say about some issue. The attack was sometimes accompanied by the words *don't judge, lest you be judged.* It's the only Bible verse most God-haters know, even though they don't have a clue about its context. It also seems to escape their notice as they hurl it at Christians, that they are at that very moment judging. The internet is a favorite hangout of the attack crowd. One particularly notorious deceiver who loves to bad mouth Christians, attacked a Christian pastor for exposing charlatans and false converts. He posted a video with a question title, which he must think is deeply profound, but which is stunningly stupid. The name of the video is *How do you know they're not Christians?* For anyone who might ever be tempted to ask such a stupid question, I have a question of my own. *How do cats know that dogs aren't cats?*

Since many Americans have expressed a desire to be deceived about political matters, it's understandable that deception in spiritual matters suits them as well. It isn't that they don't want *any* god, they just don't want *the true God.* They want the god of the TV preachers, a magic genie who is ready to fulfill our every wish. They want a god who smiles upon everything we do, much like a senile Santa Claus. And most importantly, they want a god who tells them only what they want to hear. The Apostle Paul describes a society much like ours in 2 Timothy 4:3-4: *"For the time will come when they will not endure sound doctrine, but wanting to have their ears tickled, they will accumulate for themselves teachers in accordance to their own desires; and will turn away their ears from the truth, and will turn aside to myths."*

When Jesus walked the earth, He was continually confronting religious pretenders, who put on a show of loving the Lord. They weren't much different from the pretenders of today. Here's what He said to them in Matthew 15:7-9: *"You hypocrites, rightly did Isaiah prophesy of you, saying, 'This people honors Me with their lips, But their heart is far away from Me, but in vain do they worship Me, teaching as their doctrines the precepts of men.'"*

I think we can all agree that God is bigger than us and stronger than us. This, as well as the fact that He created us, gives Him the right to lay down the Law for us. But strangely, many today don't think He has any such right. They feel that His Law isn't right and fair, and that it's a cruel imposition on their freedom. So, for those who feel this way, I suggest that they are perfectly free to order the universe any way they like, if they ever get to be God. Many seem to be campaigning for the job, but when I see the quality of the candidates, I'm very happy that it's Jesus who is running things.

Lost rebels need to know that the God they are mocking is the God we will all meet, the moment after we die. It may not be today, tomorrow, or in six months, but it's much sooner than most people think.

The delusion that we are basically good, can only be maintained if we're surrounded by sinners like us. When standing before a Judge robed in blinding holiness, there will be precious little to be proud of.

When the Judge pronounces His verdict, it will either be not guilty, or guilty. When He passes sentence, it will either be eternal heaven, or eternal hell. But the most frightening thing about the coming Judgment is that *there will be no appeal!*

A FEW THOUGHTS ABOUT HELL

We've all heard someone say *a loving God wouldn't send anyone to hell*. I tend to agree that a loving God wouldn't, but *an angry God will*. Almost everyone who I've heard voice such a sentiment has been a God-hater and an unrepentant rebel against the Lord. It's only natural that such people would desperately cling to the hope that no such place exists.

There is no Biblical doctrine that is less popular among non-believers and believers than the doctrine of hell. I'm quite certain that what I have to say about it won't make it any more popular, but I do hope that it will at least shed a little light on this dark subject.

The greatest piece of evidence that hell is real is the Bible itself. The Lord has never lied to us, and Jesus often warned His listeners about eternal punishment. The only way for hell *not* to be real is for Jesus to have lied, but that's the worst bet anyone can make.

There are disturbing deathbed accounts of some famous and not so famous atheists and God-haters, who caught a glimpse of the other side before they died. As with anything that concerns the Bible, these accounts are disputed by some living God-haters, who accuse Christians of making up such stories. However, as with any

Biblical controversy, one must consider the source. God-haters are ever busy trying to discredit the Bible, and as we've seen, they don't mind telling a few whoppers to help them accomplish that. Here are the dying words of a few individuals who ignored or mocked God:

"Oh my, oh my, what have I done, there is something very wrong.... there is something very wrong." Anton LaVey, author of the Satanic Bible and the founder of the Church of Satan

"Oh Christ! Oh Lord Jesus!....I must die – abandoned of God and of men! I shall go to hell! Oh Christ! Oh Jesus Christ!" Voltaire, French author/philosopher, known for his mocking of God and Christianity

"Oh, my nurse, my nurse! What blood, what murders, what evil counsels have I followed! Oh, my God, pardon me and have mercy on me if Thou canst. I know not what I am! What shall I do? I am lost; I see it well." Charles IX, King of France

"My God, my God, why hast thou forsaken me?....Stay with me, stay with me for God's sake. I cannot bear to be left alone!....I would give worlds, if I had them, if the Age of Reason had never been published. Oh Lord, help me! Christ, help me! It is hell to be left alone!" Thomas Paine, author, known for his mocking of God and Christianity

"That there is a God, I know, because I continually feel the effects of His wrath; that there is a hell I am equally certain....Millions and

millions of years will bring me no nearer to the end of my torments than one poor hour. Oh, eternity, eternity! Who can discover the abyss of eternity?....I have despised my Maker, and denied my Redeemer. I have joined myself to the atheist and profane, and continued this course under many convictions, till my iniquity was ripe for vengeance, and the just judgment of God overtook me when my security was the greatest, and the checks of my conscience were the least. Oh, the insufferable pangs of hell!" Sir Francis Newport, an infidel who turned his back on God early in life

"I die without hope because I insulted the Holy Spirit so bitterly. He has justly left me alone to go down to eternal night. He could not have borne with me any longer and followed farther and retained His divine honor and dignity. I wait but a few moments, and as much as I dread it, I must quit these mortal shores. I would delay, I would linger – but no! The fiends they come, Oh save me! They drag me down! Lost! Lost! Lost!" Unknown

"The devils are come, the devils are come, keep them off me! Hell and damnation, hell and damnation!" Unknown

"I am suffering the pangs of the damned." Charles Maurice de Talleyrand-Perigord, French statesman and diplomat

"Until this moment, I thought there was neither God or hell....Now I know and feel that there are both, and I am doomed to perdition by the just judgment of the Almighty." Sir Thomas Scott, Chancellor of England

I hope this is a wake-up call for lost rebels, who have deluded themselves into believing that there's no hell. There are two ways of dying, and the way we go depends on whether we're right with the Lord. An excellent book on this subject is *Dying Testimonies of the Saved and Unsaved,* by Solomon B. Shaw.

Hell is real, but why is there such a place at all? One reason for the existence of hell is that there must be a separate place for rebels. The Lord can't allow them into heaven, because they'd wage the same war there that they're waging here. Rebels must always have their own way, and just like Satan, they resent God for being God. Heaven would not be heaven with an eternal rebellion going on.

Some believe that hell is a metaphor for annihilation, because the Bible sometimes refers to it as eternal *destruction.* That might work, but the Bible also refers to it as eternal *torment,* and there's no way to fit annihilation into that. Those that read *white* when the Lord says *black,* have no problem making the Bible say anything they want, but that's a very dangerous way of reading God's Word. Once we begin to understand God's holy nature, it becomes very clear that He says what He means and means what He says. Here are a few things the Lord has said about hell:

"But for the cowardly and unbelieving and abominable and murderers and immoral persons and sorcerers and idolaters and all liars, their part will be in the lake that burns with fire and brimstone, which is the second death." Revelation 21:8

"And another angel, a third one, followed them, saying with a loud voice, 'If any one worships the beast and his image, and receives

a mark on his forehead or upon his hand, he also will drink of the wine of the wrath of God, which is mixed in full strength in the cup of His anger, and he will be tormented with fire and brimstone in the presence of the holy angels and in the presence of the Lamb. And the smoke of their torment goes up forever and ever, and they have no rest day and night, those who worship the beast and his image, and whoever receives the mark of his name.'" Revelation 14:9-11

"And I say to you, that many shall come from east and west, and recline at table with Abraham, and Isaac, and Jacob, in the kingdom of heaven; but the sons of the kingdom shall be cast into the outer darkness; in that place there shall be weeping and gnashing of teeth." Matthew 8:11-12

"And do not fear those who kill the body, but are unable to kill the soul; but rather fear Him who is able to destroy both soul and body in hell." Matthew 10:28

"Then He will also say to those on His left, 'Depart from Me, accursed ones, into the eternal fire which has been prepared for the devil and his angels.'" Matthew 25:41

"Upon the wicked He will rain snares; Fire and brimstone and burning wind will be the portion of their cup." Psalm 11:6

"And the devil who deceived them was thrown into the lake of fire and brimstone, where the beast and the false prophet are also; and they will be tormented day and night forever and ever." Revelation 20:10

"Now there was a certain rich man, and he habitually dressed in purple and fine linen, gaily living in splendor every day. And a certain poor man named Lazarus was laid at his gate, covered with sores, and longing to be fed with the crumbs which were falling from the rich man's table; besides, even the dogs were coming and licking his sores. Now it came about that the poor man died and he was carried away by the angels to Abraham's bosom; and the rich man also died and was buried. And in Hades he lifted up his eyes, being in torment, and saw Abraham far away, and Lazarus in his bosom. And he cried out and said, 'Father Abraham, have mercy on me, and send Lazarus, that he may dip the tip of his finger in water and cool off my tongue, for I am in agony in this flame.' But Abraham said, 'Child, remember that during your life you received your good things, and likewise Lazarus bad things; but now he is being comforted here, and you are in agony. And besides all this, between us and you there is a great chasm fixed, in order that those who wish to come over from here to you may not be able, and that none may cross over from there to us.' And he said, 'Then I beg you, Father, that you send him to my father's house – for I have five brothers – that he may warn them, lest they also come to this place of torment.' But Abraham said, 'They have Moses and the Prophets; let them hear them.' But he said, 'No, Father Abraham, but if someone goes to them from the dead, they will repent!' But he said to him, 'If they do not listen to Moses and the Prophets, neither will they be persuaded if someone rises from the dead.'" Luke 16:19-31

It's important for people to know about the infinite love of God, but not to the exclusion of all His other attributes. The Lord is also a God of infinite power, infinite justice, and infinite wrath. Infinity is a concept that is totally foreign to us, but God has provided us with a visual example that might help us out. This visual example should also give us an idea of how significant He is, and how insignificant we are. I made reference to the universe in the first chapter, but what is its actual size? The most recent estimates for the size of the universe is at least 94 billion light years! To gain an understanding of how large that is, please consider the following: The speed of light is approximately 186,000 miles per second, which is approximately 6 trillion miles a year. If we multiply 6 trillion miles by 94 billion, we should be getting close to the minimum size of the universe. This should dispel many of the silly notions that most people have about God, and give us a much clearer picture of who He is. It should cause us to stand in awe of Him, and think twice before mocking or challenging Him. The Bible makes the following contrast between all mankind and the Lord in Isaiah 40:17: *"All the nations are as nothing before Him, They are regarded by Him as less than nothing and meaningless."* Those who strut around like peacocks, full of their own self-importance, would do well to look up at the night sky, and see the power and glory of the Lord.

People should also consider that the Lord doesn't owe us a thing, yet He bountifully showers us with gifts and blessings from cradle to grave. His common grace blessings include such things as a breath of fresh air, a cool drink of water, food for our hunger and enjoyment, the singing of birds, restful sleep, the laughter of children, a kind and uplifting word, a beautiful song, a beautiful sunset, a sweet-smelling flower, the list is endless. But most people are completely oblivious of the fact that *all* the good that we experience in our lives comes from the hand of the Lord. Most of the torments of hell are simply the complete absence of any of the

Lord's blessings. All their lives, rebels have told God that they don't want Him, and in the end, He will honor their wish for eternity.

It needs to be stated very emphatically that God doesn't want *anyone* to go to hell. This is clear from a multitude of Scripture verses like these:

"'Do I have any pleasure in the death of the wicked,' declares the Lord God, 'rather than that he should turn from his ways and live?'" Ezekiel 18:23

"'Say to them, As I live!' declares the Lord God, 'I take no pleasure in the death of the wicked, but rather that the wicked turn from his way and live. Turn back, turn back from your evil ways! Why then will you die, O house of Israel?'" Ezekiel 33:11

"who desires all men to be saved and to come to the knowledge of the truth." 1 Timothy 2:4

"The Lord is not slow about His promise, as some count slowness, but is patient toward you, not wishing for any to perish but for all to come to repentance." 2 Peter 3:9

"For this is the will of My Father, that every one who beholds the Son, and believes in Him, may have eternal life; and I Myself will raise him up on the last day." John 6:40

"For God so loved the world, that He gave His only begotten Son, that whoever believes in Him should not perish, but have eternal life." John 3:16

From the day we're born, the Lord speaks to all of us. He speaks to us through conscience, creation, His written Word, circumstances, and people. Sometimes He whispers and sometimes He thunders, but He never ceases instructing sinners. The Bible passage that best describes the Lord's lifelong communication with sinners and the consequences of either obeying or not obeying Him is Proverbs 1:20-33: *"Wisdom shouts in the street, She lifts her voice in the square; At the head of the noisy streets she cries out; At the entrance of the gates in the city, she utters her sayings: 'How long, O naive ones, will you love simplicity? And scoffers delight themselves in scoffing, And fools hate knowledge? Turn to my reproof, Behold I will pour out my spirit on you; I will make my words known to you. Because I called, and you refused; I stretched out my hand, and no one paid attention; And you neglected all my counsel, And did not want my reproof; I will even laugh at your calamity; I will mock when your dread comes, When your dread comes like a storm, And your calamity comes on like a whirlwind, When distress and anguish come on you. Then they will call on me, but I will not answer; They will seek me diligently, but they shall not find me, Because they hated knowledge, and did not choose the fear of the Lord. They would not accept my counsel, They spurned all my reproof. So they shall eat of the fruit of their own way, And be satiated with their own devices. For the waywardness of the naive shall kill them, And the complacency of fools shall destroy them. But he who listens to me shall live securely, And shall be at ease from the dread of evil.'"*

A very common objection to Christianity is that everyone hasn't had the opportunity to hear the Gospel. This is absolutely true, but everyone doesn't *need* to hear the Gospel. If people already reject the light they have, they will also reject the greater light of the Gospel. On the other hand, if people respond positively to the light they have, God will grant them more light. Missionary history is full of stories of solitary individuals coming to the Lord in some remote part of the world. God is intimately acquainted with all His creatures, and He can reach anyone, anywhere, at any time. There's a beautiful picture in Revelation 5:9, which shows that God's salvation is available to all: *"And they sang a new song, saying, 'Worthy art Thou to take the book, and to break its seals; for Thou wast slain, and didst purchase for God with Thy blood men from every tribe and tongue and people and nation.'"*

We were all *born* rebels, but we don't have to *stay* rebels. What ultimately sends people to hell is lifelong rejection of light and unceasing rebellion against the Lord. Individually and collectively, people have a natural affinity for darkness and have been trying to dethrone God for approximately six thousand years. This of course is a fool's errand, because even mankind's collective effort has had an infinitely smaller chance of succeeding than a flea would have in bringing down an elephant. Nevertheless, the majority of mankind is now in the process of mounting a final, monumental, and ultimately futile challenge against the Lord. It is the challenge we read about in the book of Revelation, and it will end exactly the way the book prophesies. Some may wish to get right with the Lord and avoid the fate that awaits all rebels.

A GRACIOUS INVITATION FROM A LOVING GOD

I'm glad you've made it to the final chapter. We may have left a few stragglers behind, because the Word of God tells us that lost sinners love darkness and lies. Our fallen human nature craves these things, but the only hope for a broken society and for broken people is truth.

Adam and Eve severed their relationship with the Lord through self-will and pride, and they passed on their lost condition to all of us. In order for the relationship with the Lord to be restored, our course must be reversed. The opposite of self-will is submitting to the will of the Lord, and the opposite of pride is humility. Satan tells people that self-will and pride will bring them freedom, but that freedom eventually ends up enslaving them. The Lord calls us instead to humble ourselves and submit to *His* will, but these liberate.

The devil always sugarcoats his lies, but the Lord never sugarcoats the truth. According to the father of lies, man is a virtuous being who has evolved to heights of glory, and there's no need for him to examine himself. The Lord tells us that we are all born wicked and depraved, and that we should examine not only ourselves, but mankind in general. Only a cursory examination of mankind will show that we are destroying the earth and treating each other worse than animals treat their own kind. The 20th century was the bloodiest and most depraved century in human history. That looks more like devolution than evolution. If animals could build things, they'd have no need to build insane asylums and prisons, because man is the only creature that's sick in the head, sick in the heart, and out of control.

We've already seen what God's Word says about all of us, and it is confirmed by what we see all around us. In Romans 3:23, we read that *"all have sinned and fall short of the glory of God."* Because God's justice demands that sin be punished, in Romans 6:23, we read that *"the wages of sin is death."* Many people have been deceived into believing that if our good deeds outweigh our evil deeds, God will grant us entrance into heaven. This is categorically not true. The Lord gives us the most extreme example of good deeds outweighing evil deeds in the book of James 2:10, and even that falls way short. *"For whoever keeps the whole law and yet stumbles in one point, he has become guilty of all."* So much for trying to earn our way to heaven.

What a hopeless situation to be in, knowing that no matter how much good we do, it will never be enough. There *are* counterfeit forms of Christianity, which teach that we can earn our way to heaven, but we must make a choice. Do we believe people, or do we believe God? There are many Bible passages which teach that salvation *cannot* be earned. Perhaps the clearest of those passages can be found in the book of Ephesians 2:8-9, where we read *"For by grace you have been saved through faith; and that not of yourselves, it is the gift of God; not as a result of works, that no one should boast."*

We saw in the Garden of Eden account that after Adam and Eve sinned and realized what they had done, they sewed fig leaves together to cover their nakedness. But their own efforts couldn't adequately cover their sin, so the Lord made garments of skin for them. An animal had to die as their substitute, which symbolized the coming Messiah who would die in the place of sinners. Speaking of John the Baptist, this is what the Gospel of John 1:29 says: *"The next day he saw Jesus coming to him, and said 'Behold the Lamb of God who takes away the sin of the world.'"*

Many believe that Jesus' mission on earth was to teach us truth and morality. He certainly did that, and He is without a doubt the greatest moral teacher who ever lived, but the main reason He came to earth was to die for the sins of mankind. Our sin debt to God is so great, only God Himself could pay that debt. The Old Testament is full of prophecies about the coming Savior who would die for our sins, but one passage stands out. This is what Isaiah 53:4-7 says: *"Surely our griefs He Himself bore, And our sorrows He carried; Yet we ourselves esteemed Him stricken, Smitten of God, and afflicted. But He was pierced through for our transgressions, He was crushed for our iniquities; The chastening for our well-being fell upon Him, And by His scourging we are healed. All of us like sheep have gone astray, Each of us has turned to his own way; But the Lord has caused the iniquity of us all to fall upon Him. He was oppressed and He was afflicted, Yet He did not open His mouth; Like a lamb that is led to slaughter, And like a sheep that is silent before its shearers, So He did not open His mouth."*

The crucifixion of Jesus Christ was a stunning historical event, and it leaves us all with a choice. Do we believe in Jesus' substitutionary death for us and put our trust in His sacrifice to save us, or do we trust in our own goodness to save us? Genuine faith is one which recognizes that we are utterly lost, with absolutely no hope of earning salvation. It's one condition for entering God's kingdom. Another condition is repentance.

The subject of repentance is almost as unpopular as the subject of hell, so it's almost never mentioned in most churches. However, it's just as essential for salvation as faith. The Old Testament prophets continually called people to repentance. John the Baptist, the Apostles, and Jesus called people to repentance as well. Here are a few Scripture verses that emphasize the importance of repentance:

"Therefore say to the house of Israel, 'Thus says the Lord God, Repent and turn away from your idols, and turn your faces away from all your abominations.'" Ezekiel 14:6

"But the house of Israel says, 'The way of the Lord is not right.' 'Are my ways not right, O house of Israel? Is it not your ways that are not right? Therefore I will judge you , O house of Israel, each according to his conduct,' declares the Lord God. 'Repent and turn away from all your transgressions, so that iniquity may not be a stumbling block to you. Cast away from you all your transgressions which you have committed, and make yourselves a new heart and a new spirit! For why will you die, O house of Israel? For I have no pleasure in the death of anyone who dies,' declares the Lord God. 'Therefore, repent and live.'" Ezekiel 18:29-32

"Let the wicked forsake his way, And the unrighteous man his thoughts; And let him return to the Lord, And He will have compassion on him; And to our God, For He will abundantly pardon." Isaiah 55:7

"O Lord, do not Thine eyes look for truth? Thou hast smitten them, But they did not weaken; Thou hast consumed them, But they refused to take correction. They have made their faces harder than rock; They have refused to repent." Jeremiah 5:3

"Now in those days John the Baptist came, preaching in the wilderness of Judea, saying, 'Repent, for the kingdom of heaven is at hand.'" Matthew 3:1-2

"From that time Jesus began to preach and say, 'Repent, for the kingdom of heaven is at hand.'" Matthew 4:17

"Then He began to reproach the cities in which most of His miracles were done, because they did not repent. 'Woe to you, Chorazin! Woe to you, Bethsaida! For if the miracles had occurred in Tyre and Sidon which occurred in you, they would have repented long ago in sackcloth and ashes. Nevertheless I say to you, it shall be more tolerable for Tyre and Sidon in the day of judgment, than for you. And you, Capernaum, will not be exalted to heaven, will you? You shall descend down to Hades; for if the miracles had occurred in Sodom which occurred in you, it would have remained to this day. Nevertheless I say to you that it shall be more tolerable for the land of Sodom in the day of judgment, than for you.'" Matthew 11:20-24

"And after John had been taken into custody, Jesus came into Galilee, preaching the gospel of God, and saying, 'The time is fulfilled, and the kingdom of God is at hand; repent and believe in the gospel.'" Mark 1:14-15

"And they went out and preached that men should repent." Mark 6:12

"And Peter said to them, 'Repent, and let each of you be baptized in the name of Jesus Christ for the forgiveness of your sins; and you shall receive the gift of the Holy Spirit.'" Acts 2:38

"Repent therefore and return, that your sins may be wiped away, in order that times of refreshing may come from the presence of the Lord." Acts 3:19

"Therefore having overlooked the times of ignorance, God is now declaring to men that all everywhere should repent, because He has fixed a day in which He will judge the world in righteousness through a Man whom He has appointed, having furnished proof to all men by raising Him from the dead." Acts 17:30-31

So, what does the word "repentance" mean? The Hebrew and Greek words in the Bible that have been translated into the English word "repentance" are remorse, regret, changing one's mind, turning around and going in the opposite direction. This is the type of attitude and mindset the Lord requires of us, and that explains why the word "repentance" has practically been eliminated from our vocabulary. It's precisely the type of attitude and mindset most people don't want.

We've read in the Ephesians passage that salvation is free, and in the sense that there's nothing we can do to earn it, that's absolutely true. But to say that following the Lord doesn't cost anything is an absolute lie. Seeing ourselves as the Lord sees us and repenting will automatically cost us our pride. Seeing our own wretchedness and giving up our own will for His are the most humbling things proud sinners can do. Following the Lord may also cost us the approval of our family, our friends, and society at large.

One false idea which has become popular in recent years is that repentance is a work, and that it therefore nullifies faith. The truth of the matter is that faith and repentance are essentially two sides of the same coin. If we have genuine faith in the God who calls us to repentance, then the natural result of that type of faith *will* be repentance. If we repent, it's simply an outward manifestation of genuine faith residing in us. There is no contradiction, and neither one of these nullifies the other.

As word of Jesus' miracles spread throughout the countryside, the crowds got bigger and bigger, sometimes numbering in the thousands. At His crucifixion, His true followers numbered a few hundred. People in Jesus' day were no different than people today. They loved the miracles, but most of them didn't care for Jesus' teaching about the cost of true discipleship. Anyone who wishes to enter God's kingdom should listen to the words of Jesus when He tells us the cost:

"Every one therefore who shall confess Me before men, I will also confess him before My Father who is in heaven. But whoever shall deny Me before men, I will also deny him before My Father who is in heaven. Do not think that I came to bring peace on the earth; I did not come to bring peace, but a sword. For I came to set a man against his father, and a daughter against her mother, and a daughter-in-law against her mother-in-law; and a man's enemies will be the members

of his household. He who loves father or mother more than Me is not worthy of Me; and he who loves son or daughter more than Me is not worthy of Me. And he who does not take his cross and follow after Me is not worthy of Me. He who has found his life shall lose it, and he who has lost his life for My sake shall find it." Matthew 10:32-39

"And He summoned the multitude with His disciples, and said to them, 'If anyone wishes to come after Me, let him deny himself, and take up his cross, and follow Me. For whoever wishes to save his life shall lose it; and whoever loses his life for My sake and the gospel's shall save it. For what does it profit a man to gain the whole world, and forfeit his soul? For what shall a man give in exchange for his soul? For whoever is ashamed of Me and My words in this adulterous and sinful generation, the Son of Man will also be ashamed of him when He comes in the glory of His Father with the holy angels.'" Mark 8:34-38

It becomes clear from Scriptures such as these that there's more to being a genuine Christian than most people were led to believe. Rather than simply reciting a prayer about accepting Jesus into our hearts, the Lord is asking us to lay down our lives for Him. He is our Creator, and it's only right that our love for Him be greater than our love for anything else. The people closest to us, our possessions, and even our very lives, are all just gifts He has given to us. Should we love the gifts more than the Giver?

It's important to remember that while we can fool ourselves and others, there is no fooling God. I'd like to share the clearest teaching of Jesus about those who are true believers, and those who only think they are. It comes from the Gospel of Matthew:

"Enter by the narrow gate; for the gate is wide, and the way is broad that leads to destruction, and many are those who enter by it. For the gate is small, and the way is narrow that leads to life, and few are those who find it. Beware of the false prophets, who come to you in sheep's clothing, but inwardly are ravenous wolves. You will know them by their fruits. Grapes are not gathered from thorn bushes, nor figs from thistles, are they? Even so, every good tree bears good fruit; but the rotten tree bears bad fruit. A good tree cannot produce bad fruit, nor can a rotten tree produce good fruit. Every tree that does not bear good fruit is cut down and thrown into the fire. So then, you will know them by their fruits. Not every one who says to Me, 'Lord, Lord,' will enter the kingdom of heaven; but he who does the will of My Father who is in heaven. Many will say to Me on that day, 'Lord, Lord, did we not prophesy in Your name, and in Your name cast out demons, and in Your name perform many miracles?' And then I will declare to them, 'I never knew you; depart from Me, you who practice lawlessness.' Therefore every one who hears these words of Mine, and acts upon them, may be compared to a wise man, who built his house upon the rock. And the rain descended, and the floods came, and the winds blew, and burst against that house; and yet it did not fall, for it had been founded upon the rock. And every one who hears these words of Mine, and does not act upon them, will be like a foolish man, who built his house upon the sand. And the rain descended, and the floods came, and the winds blew, and burst against that house; and it fell, and great was its fall." Matthew 7:13-27

In this passage, Jesus contradicts the notion that spiritual truth can be found where the biggest crowd is. In fact, He tells us very plainly that *many* are on the way to destruction. The broad way doesn't have a signpost saying *Destination Hell*, but that's where it's going. He also tells us that *few* find the narrow way and the small gate which lead to life. This is a sobering thought, and it should motivate us to seek both of them earnestly. Next, Jesus tells us to beware of false prophets who come dressed as sheep. I've often heard people remark about how certain religious con artists look and sound so honest. That of course is the whole point of Jesus' warning. Deceivers don't come with signs on their foreheads that say *Deceiver*. The Lord then gives us a glimpse of Judgment Day. There will be those that performed certain religious activities in the name of Jesus, who will be told to depart from the Lord. The reason Jesus gives is that He never knew them, which is another way of saying that they never knew Him. And finally, Jesus gives us an illustration of two house builders. One built his house on the rock and the other one on sand. Both houses probably looked the same, but when the storm came, one stood and the other one fell. The only difference between the houses were their foundations. Both house builders *heard* the words of Jesus, but only one *acted* upon them.

The words of Jesus can be found in the four Gospels, and since He is God, they can also be found on every page of the Bible. If you ever run across anyone who accepts certain parts of Holy Scripture and rejects others, then you've just found a counterfeit Christian. Should that person be in a pulpit, then you've just found a wolf in sheep's clothing. If you care about your immortal soul, don't just walk away, *run!*

It would go way beyond the scope of this book to name every major cult and every well-known deceiver. The *Helpful Resources* section at the end of the book will be useful for that. Right now, the best that I can do is provide a little guidance to anyone who wants to get right with the Lord. The place to start is to have a heart to heart talk with our heavenly Father.

It doesn't matter who you are, where you are, or what you've done. You may have been the worst of rebels, but if you're genuinely heart-broken for offending the Lord and wish to commit your life to Him, He has promised to forgive you, to grant you eternal life, and to empower you to serve Him. Just confess your sins and repent, ask for His mercy, and put your trust in the sacrifice of Jesus.

The next thing is to open the Bible and to allow the Lord to talk to *you*. When looking for a church, the most important thing is to find one where the Word of God isn't just a decoration, but is believed and taught from cover to cover. Some churches are nothing more than theater, featuring ridiculous costumes, ridiculous clergy titles, ridiculous rituals and ceremonies, and ridiculous teaching that can be found nowhere in the Bible. It's best to avoid such churches. These are some of the clearest indications of spiritual bankruptcy and pretension, because genuine believers have no need to put on a show. In fact, the Lord forbids us from doing so. A building may have a cross on the door or the roof, but that doesn't mean it's a Christian church. It may very well be a cult. It's also good to remember that even in the best churches, there are some who love the Lord and some who are pretenders. We don't have to worry about the pretenders, the Lord will deal with them. Our job is to make sure that *we* aren't pretenders. The most dangerous deception of all is *self-deception*.

In closing, I'd like to share a powerful story about pretenders, which illustrates what it means to be a real Christian. Years ago, I heard a sermon in which the preacher told this story. It took place in a small village church in Russia, in the days of the old Soviet Union. In the middle of the church service, a number of soldiers broke into the church, and turned their machine guns on the congregation. Here's a rough summary of what they said to the people: *"You filthy Christians! You are a blight on our Motherland and on our glorious Communist Revolution! You don't deserve to live, and we're here to make sure that you die! However, there may be some among you who don't believe all this Christian superstition, and if you are one of those, we will give you sixty seconds to leave the building."* One by one, people got up and began heading for the door. When the last person left and more than half the congregation was gone, the soldiers laid down their guns and one of them said, *"brothers, we have come to worship Christ with you, but we first had to get rid of the hypocrites."*

It's very easy to profess to be a Christian when it costs absolutely nothing. It's even easier when it might be a benefit to one's reputation, one's business, or one's political ambitions. But how many will profess their faith in Jesus Christ when it begins to cost something? And, how many will still profess their faith in Him when it is certain to cost them their lives?

Over the last twenty centuries, millions of Christians have paid the ultimate price for their faith in the Lord. Many more than that were only playing church, and turned their backs on the Lord when the cost became too high. Jesus told us clearly that the pretenders would be *many*, and that the faithful would be *few*. May we be among the few.

Finally, here are some words from early Protestant Reformer John Hus, who was one of those that paid the ultimate price: *"Seek the truth, listen to the truth, teach the truth, love the truth, abide by the truth, and defend the truth unto death."* The greatest truth of all is that God Himself came to earth. He was born in a stable, lived a sinless life, shed His blood on a cross to pay for our sins, and He rose from the grave on the third day. He invites all to come to Him and live. For those who hear His voice, here are a few Scripture verses to help you on your journey:

"....it is appointed for men to die once, and after this comes judgment." Hebrews 9:27

"....God is opposed to the proud, but gives grace to the humble." James 4:6

"The fear of the Lord is the beginning of wisdom, And knowledge of the Holy One is understanding." Proverbs 9:10

"The fear of man brings a snare, But he who trusts in the Lord will be exalted." Proverbs 29:25

"Truly I say to you, unless you are converted and become like children, you shall not enter the kingdom of heaven." Matthew 18:3

"Do not think that I came to abolish the Law or the Prophets; I did not come to abolish, but to fulfill. For truly I say to you, until heaven and earth pass away, not the smallest letter or stroke shall pass away from the Law, until all is accomplished." Matthew 5:17-18

"Jesus said to him, 'I am the way, and the truth, and the life; no one comes to the Father, but through Me.'" John 14:6

"The thief comes only to steal, and kill, and destroy; I came that they might have life, and might have it abundantly. I am the good shepherd; the good shepherd lays down His life for the sheep." John 10:10-11

"Come to Me, all who are weary and heavy-laden, and I will give you rest. Take my yoke upon you, and learn from Me, for I am gentle and humble in heart; and you shall find rest for your souls." Matthew 11:28-29

"Again therefore Jesus spoke to them, saying, 'I am the light of the world; he who follows Me shall not walk in the darkness, but shall have the light of life.'" John 8:12

"He who trusts in his own heart is a fool." Proverbs 28:26

"He who justifies the wicked, and he who condemns the righteous, Both of them alike are an abomination to the Lord." Proverbs 17:15

"Do not let kindness and truth leave you; Bind them around your neck, Write them on the tablet of your heart." Proverbs 3:3

"He who has My commandments and keeps them, he it is who loves Me; and he who loves Me shall be loved by My Father, and I will love him, and will disclose Myself to him." John 14:21

"And the Lord is the one who goes ahead of you; He will be with you. He will not fail you or forsake you. Do not fear, or be dismayed." Deuteronomy 31:8

"Jesus therefore was saying to those Jews who had believed Him, 'If you abide in My word, then you are truly disciples of Mine; and you shall know the truth, and the truth shall make you free.'" John 8:31-32

AFTERWORD ABOUT COVID

Today, we are deep into the vaccine stage of the Covid operation. The results of this operation have been devastating, but not nearly as devastating as its architects had intended. Many of the initially confused have awakened to the deception, but most who started lost in 2020 are unfortunately still lost. The following pages are a brief summary of the deception, and it will hopefully awaken a few more lost souls.

The deceivers have exposed themselves in a thousand ways, but the talking box has authenticated their lies. The sheeple do of course love fairy tales, and they know that the talking box is never wrong. In the context of the Covid operation, the two have had the perfect sadomasochistic relationship. The deceivers have essentially said *we'd like to inflict some pain, cruelty, and humiliation on you, and the sheeple have said yes, please do, and could we please have a double portion?*

Since the start of 2020, we have seen great evil and great gullibility, and discerning Christians are the only people on the planet who know what is still to come. It can come a little sooner, or a little later, depending on how many sheeple wake up in the very near future.

The deceivers have been peddling ridiculous absurdities from the start of the Covid operation. Initially, they stated that masks only offer the illusion of protection, which in fact happens to be the truth, but a short time later they stated that masks are essential and mandated them. They told us that people should be wearing two, and even *three* masks. They told us that there are about 4,000 Covid variants. They told us that 80% of the deer population is infected with Covid. They even stated that artificial vaccine immunity is much better than natural immunity. These are the type of absurdities we have been subjected to for years.

Unfortunately for many sheeple, no number of absurdities will be enough to wake them up, and no number of facts will be enough to wake them up. There are two major reasons for this. First of all, the ugly truth and its shocking implications terrifies many of them. As a result, they will desperately cling to anything and everything the deceivers say to explain away all the absurdities and all the facts. Most sheeple have the mindset of little children. They see the world as one full of kittens, puppies, butterflies, and rainbows, and they lack the maturity to recognize that in reality, the world is full of unimaginable evil. The second reason many sheeple will never wake up is that they have way too much invested in this deception, and their pride won't allow them to admit that they've fallen for such an *obvious* scam, for such a long time.

I said that the deceivers have exposed themselves in a thousand ways, but every once in a while, they've even *admitted* that they've been deceiving the public. We often heard that Covid hospitalizations were on the rise, especially among children. In order to gin up hysteria about the "pandemic," the deceivers were continually beating this drum, but what is the real story about these Covid hospitalizations? Dr. Fauci didn't give the public much truth during the height of Covid lunacy, but at one point he slipped up and hit us with a truth bomb. Here's Dr. Fauci in late December of 2021, on the topic of Covid hospitalizations: *"Many of them are hospitalized with Covid as opposed to because of Covid, and what we mean by that, if a child goes in the hospital, they automatically get tested for Covid, and they get counted as a Covid hospitalized individual, when in fact they may go in for a broken leg or appendicitis or something like that, so it's over-counting the number of children who are quote hospitalized with Covid as opposed to because of Covid."* It's a safe bet that Dr. Fauci regretted this statement the moment it left his mouth, because he inadvertently exposed a core deception of the Covid scam. Since the start of 2020, a multitude of similar deceptions have given the public the impression that we were in the middle of a pandemic.

The objective of the vaccine stage of the Covid operation was a government vaccine mandate. By the deceivers' own admission, this would not happen until they achieved 75% to 80% voluntary compliance. This presented a major challenge for them, because only about 40% of the public couldn't wait to get jabbed. The rest were either skeptical or adamantly opposed. To get the other 35% to 40%, they employed the reliable carrot and stick routine. First came the carrot of course. Free coffee and donuts, free steak dinners, free airline tickets, free movie tickets, monetary bonuses at the workplace, and even free bags of marijuana. It became amusing to watch them bribe the public to accept their magic potion. Once the carrot accomplished all it could, they ceased being so nice, and the stick appeared. Globalist businesses were of course the first to mandate the vaccine for their employees, and many smaller businesses predictably followed. The monkey see --- monkey do phenomenon has been highly instrumental in getting the scam off the ground, and in keeping it alive. Some tyrants ordered businesses to mandate the vaccine for their employees, and some even ordered businesses to turn away customers who weren't jabbed.

We've seen these mandates cause division and chaos across the nation. Essential services became critically short-staffed, due to the firing and resignation of many workers. They put an added strain on supply chains, which naturally resulted in more and more shortages. Starting in 2020, we saw the land of the free succumb to mass psychosis, and rapidly devolve into the land of tyrants, slaves, and lunatics. Some of the brutal coercion techniques we witnessed come directly from the Communist playbook. Suspicion has been mounting for quite some time about the fanatical obsession to get the Covid vaccine into everyone. Even those who have been exposed to Covid and who now have natural immunity, as well as young children for whom Covid poses almost zero risk.

Most people don't have a clue about the devastation the Covid scam has caused. As a result of the insane response to Covid by tyrants, hundreds of millions of people worldwide have been forced into extreme poverty. In the early part of 2020, a chief economist from the United Nation's World Food Program warned that 130 million people would be brought to the brink of starvation by the end of 2020 due to lockdowns. Millions of small businesses worldwide, and hundreds of thousands in America have been forced into bankruptcy. Alcoholism, drug addiction, and depression reached record levels. Suicides reached record levels. Spousal abuse, child abuse, and all other violent crimes also reached record levels.

In addition to all this, there's already a medical catastrophe in progress. It generally takes a *minimum* of five years to bring a vaccine to market. They're tested for years on guinea pigs and other animals, to make sure they're safe in the long-term. In the case of the Covid vaccine however, *we* were chosen to be the guinea pigs. We heard endless boasting about the amazingly rapid development of this vaccine, but this is the very last thing anyone should have boasted about. At best, its rapid development and almost instant approval was sheer recklessness. We've already seen what some of the *tested* vaccines have done to people. As you may recall from Robert Kennedy's Instagram post, one vaccination program in India has crippled approximately half a million children. We can't begin to imagine the final result of the medical catastrophe that has been unfolding, as a result of a vaccine which has *not* been tested.

The destruction of the world economy through lockdowns and countless other nonsensical restrictions, as well as the mandating of an untested medical product, have almost certainly brought about a death toll that is orders of magnitude greater than the death toll from Covid. Pandemic or not, the response to Covid is the most extreme example any of us have ever seen of the cure being worse than the disease.

The economic destruction that has occurred to date is more devastating than most people realize. When gauging the strength of our economy, people generally only look at the stock market. When the Dow Jones Industrial Average is at record highs, people naturally assume that things must not be so bad. Unfortunately, the performance of the stock market is an utterly irrelevant indicator of economic strength. Whenever there's more buying than selling, the market goes up, and those with an unlimited amount of money can buy like mad. If the globalists wanted, they could double the Dow Jones number in one day. Conversely, they can sell like mad and create a market crash. The market numbers are just one of their many deceptions, and because they know ahead of time what's coming, they make money whether the market soars or crashes. To see the actual state of our economy, we need to consider many other factors besides market numbers, and these clearly indicate that the economic situation is disastrous.

For a long time after the pharmaceutical companies unleashed their Covid vaccine on the world, the television ran one continuous, ridiculous vaccine commercial. If we didn't know it was poison in a needle, we might have thought that a Covid vaccine was the tastiest candy that has ever hit the market. We also might have thought that allowing ourselves to be injected would bring joy and inspiration to others, because we saw that when grandma received her shot, there was a crowd gathered around, giving her a rousing round of applause. To make the poison even more palatable, every shill from New York to California endlessly assured us that it's perfectly safe. The sheeple never ask any questions, but if they ever do, they should ask this one: *How can anyone possibly guarantee the long-term safety of a vaccine that hasn't undergone long-term safety trials?*

In any case, even the short-term safety of the vaccine has long been in question. Some people have had no adverse health affects, some became mildly sick, some became violently sick, some have been crippled for life, and some have died. The death count began as soon as the first guinea pigs got their shots. When people first became aware of this, the deceivers began frantically assuring the public that the vaccine was definitely *not* the cause of those deaths. A person may have just died and the deceivers may have been hundreds of miles away, but they *knew* that the death wasn't caused by the vaccine.

The reports about the Covid vaccine have been so disturbing, it may be time to take a closer look at the so-called pandemic we've been forced to go through and to start asking some serious questions. For example, was the created hysteria the least bit justified? Was the destruction of the economy justified? Who benefited from the hysteria and the destruction? Why were doctors who even questioned the official Covid narrative viciously attacked? Was it mere coincidence that *all* the major pharmaceutical companies miraculously came up with a vaccine at the same time? Those who think critically can come up with more questions, and each one of those questions will be like a piece in a jigsaw puzzle that will reveal the true picture of what happened to us in 2020 and the years following.

There are times when we can be looking at things and still not see them, unless someone points them out to us. There are of course other times, when all the help in the world doesn't help us see, because we don't really *want* to see. For those who do want to see the things which are right in front of their eyes, I will make a few final observations.

As of September 21, 2023, the reported worldwide death toll from Covid according to the WHO's own website was 6,958,499. India's reported death toll as of that day was 532,030, and China's reported death toll was 121,679. Finally, America's reported death toll as of that day was 1,127,152. Can anyone see any problems with these numbers? It comes down to a simple math equation if we know what percentage of the world's population lives in America. That number is 4.23%, which means America must have approximately 4.23% of the world's Covid deaths, give or take a percentage point. That comes to 294,344, which is nowhere near 1,127,152. Looking at it another way, the combined population of India and China is a little more than 2.8 billion, which is about eight times greater than the population of America, and yet their combined Covid death toll is only about half of America's.

Doesn't a single journalist in America have access to a calculator? Furthermore, does *any* person seriously believe that a nation whose population is 4.23% of the world's population, has had more than 16% of the world's Covid deaths? It seems to me that it's much easier to believe a multitude of doctors who blew the whistle on a massive cause of death fraud that they were asked to participate in by the CDC. Those who still doubt can look at the official death toll for the flu virus for the 2020-2021 season. It seems that almost no one died from the flu that season. From the time Covid appeared until the arrival of the vaccine, there seems to have been a precipitous drop in deaths from all other diseases. When added up, this drop in deaths in that particular time period will give us a number that is roughly equivalent to the reported death toll from Covid in the same time period. When the vaccine arrived, the overall mortality rate in America began to skyrocket.

In summation, it should be obvious to all by now that no effort has been spared to create the *illusion* of a disease pandemic of epic proportions. However, after considering all the facts presented in this book, does any rational and objective person still think that the Covid outbreak is anything that resembles a pandemic of epic proportions, or any kind of pandemic? The powers that be and their agents have been telling us since the start of 2020 that we should believe *them*, and not our own lying eyes. But those who choose to believe their own eyes should have no problem seeing the huge difference between a pandemic and an attempted political takeover.

I believe it's safe to assume that most of the Covid facts in this book are common knowledge to *all* our elected representatives, *all* our health "experts," *all* journalists, and *all* media personalities. So, here's a question *all* of us might ask *all* of those who have been deceiving the public so long, and who thereby ensured so much death and destruction: *What did you hope to gain from all your deceptions?* We already have a fairly good idea, but the world would still like to hear your answer.

The Covid show has had an extraordinarily good run. A much better run in fact than it ever deserved. The silly props, the bad acting, and the poorly written, monotonous, and nonsensical script should have brought down the curtain on this farce before the end of 2020. In Hans Christian Andersen's story about the vanity of an emperor and the gullibility of people, the truth that the emperor was naked as a jaybird eventually dawned on everyone. In a similar fashion, the truth about Covid is beginning to dawn on more people every day, despite all efforts of all professional liars.

HELPFUL RESOURCES

Recommending certain people as helpful sources of truth is not to be construed as endorsing everything those people have ever said or written, because no one is or can be absolutely right about everything. Discernment is called for when using this resource list. When it comes to Bible teachers, what is most important is that they have a grasp of the essentials of the Christian faith. The non-essentials, Christians are free to disagree about. As in all things, we should be discerning and diligently study God's Word ourselves.

DOCUMENTARIES

God Of Wonders
The Case For A Creator
The Case For Christ
American Gospel: Christ Alone
American Gospel: Christ Crucified
The Atheist Delusion
Ten Of The Top Scientific Facts In The Bible
Incredible Creatures That Defy Evolution – Parts 1, 2 & 3
Evolution vs God

Is Genesis History?

The Best Movie Explaining Noah's Flood Ever Made

The Ark And The Darkness

The Search For The Real Mt. Sinai

The Exodus Revealed: Searching For The Red Sea Crossing

Plandemic

The Real Anthony Fauci Movie

The Great Awakening (2023) Full Documentary

Fauci Unmasked

Vaxxed: From Cover-Up To Catastrophe

Vaxxed II: The People's Truth

Vaccine Nation

The Truth About Bill Gates (Full Corbett Documentary)

The Truth About Bill Gates 4 – Part Documentary

Big Pharma Big Money: Documentary On The Money And
Corruption Of Big Pharmaceutical Companies

What Is A Woman?

Am I Racist?

Police State 2023 Full Movie

Death Of A Nation

Hillary's America: The Secret History Of The Democratic Party

Will You Go To Hell For Me?

Best 9/11 Documentary Ever Full Movie

The Great Conspiracy: The 9/11 Special You Never Saw

Loose Change 2nd Edition Full Movie

JFK To 9/11 Everything Is A Rich Man's Trick

The New Pearl Harbor – Best 9/11 Documentary

Naudet Brothers 9/11 Documentary

9/11: Press For Truth

9/11 Was An Inside Job – Truth Without Colors

America: Freedom To Fascism

Camp FEMA

The Essential Church Movie

The Submerging Church

The Church Of Tares

Expelled

The Hidden Faith Of The Founding Fathers

A Lamp In The Dark – The Untold History Of The Bible

Third Adam

Third Adam 2

Third Adam 3

Third Adam 4

The One Question To End Abortion – What Is It?

"180" Movie

Life After Abortion

BOOKS

Mere Christianity/C.S. Lewis

Pilgrim's Progress/John Bunyan

The Law/Frederic Bastiat

Foxe's Book Of Martyrs/John Foxe

The Truth War/John MacArthur

The Great Covid Deception/Billy Crone

The Real Anthony Fauci: Bill Gates, Big Pharma, And
The Global War On Democracy And Public Health/
Robert F. Kennedy Jr.

"Cause Unknown": The Epidemic Of Sudden Deaths
In 2021 And 2022/Edward Dowd

Fault Lines/Voddie T. Baucham Jr.

The Big Lie: Exposing The Nazi Roots Of The
American Left/Dinesh D'Souza

25 Lies: Exposing Democrats' Most Dangerous, Seductive,
Damnable, Destructive Lies And How To Refute Them/
Vince Everett Ellison

Crime Inc.: How Democrats Employ Mafia And Gangster
Tactics To Gain And Hold Power/
Vince Everett Ellison

Battle For The American Mind/Pete Hegseth

Killing The Planet: How A Financial Cartel Doomed
Mankind/Rodney Howard-Browne

I Don't Have Enough Faith To Be An Atheist/
Norman L. Geisler and Frank Turek

Correct, Not Politically Correct/Frank Turek

Stealing From God/Frank Turek

Cold Case Christianity/J. Warner Wallace

Irreversible Damage/Abigail Shrier

Awake, Not Woke/Noelle Mering

American Marxism/Mark Levin

Darwin's Doubt/Stephen C. Meyer

One Race One Blood/Ken Ham and A. Charles Ware

Six Days/Ken Ham

Tower Of Babel/Bodie Hodge

Replacing Darwin/Dr. Nathaniel T. Jeanson

Many Infallible Proofs/Henry M. Morris

The Genesis Flood/John C. Whitcomb and Henry M. Morris

Worlds In Collision/Immanuel Velikovsky

Darwin's Black Box: The Biochemical Challenge
To Evolution/Michael J. Behe

Keeping Faith In An Age Of Reason/Jason Lisle

Evidence That Demands A Verdict/Josh McDowell

Another Gospel?/Alisa Childers

Letter To The American Church/Eric Metaxas

What If Jesus Had Never Been Born?/D. James Kennedy

My Life Without God/William J. Murray

How I Found Freedom In An Unfree World/Harry Browne

The Gold Of Exodus/Howard Blum

Plague Of Corruption/Judy Mikovits

The Creature From Jekyll Island/G. Edward Griffin

The New Pearl Harbor/David Ray Griffin

Debunking 9/11 Debunking/David Ray Griffin

Dying Testimonies Of The Saved And Unsaved/Solomon B. Shaw

The Kingdom Of The Cults/Walter Martin

TRUTH CHANNELS, PODCASTS, AND WEBSITES

Grace To You/John MacArthur

Answers In Genesis/Ken Ham

Answers In Genesis Canada/Calvin Smith

Justin Peters Ministries

Tucker Carlson Network (TCN)/Tucker Carlson

Biblical Science Institute/Jason Lisle

Living Waters/Ray Comfort

G3 Ministries

Relatable/Allie Beth Stuckey

The Briefing/Abert Mohler

CrossExamined/Frank Turek

Voddie Baucham

Proclaiming The Gospel/Mike Gendron

Pastor Michael Grant

The Messed Up Church/Steven Kozar

James White

Steve Deace

Mike Winger

Kent Hovind

Doug Wilson

Gary Hamrick

Costi Hinn

Allen Jackson Ministries

Larry Alex Taunton

Cold Case Christianity/J. Warner Wallace

Daily Wire/Ben Shapiro, Matt Walsh,
Michael Knowles, Andrew Klavan

Sky News Australia

Chuck Missler

Dinesh D'Souza

Fight For Truth/Colin Miller

A Call For An Uprising

Sowell Explains/Thomas Sowell

Institute For Creation Research

Olive Tree Ministries/Jan Markell

Hope For Our Times/Tom Hughes

The Watchman/Erick Stakelbeck

Martyn Iles

Dr. James Tour

PragerU

Eric Metaxas

Sean McDowell

Alisa Childers

Doreen Virtue

Becket Cook

Greg Koukl

Polite Leader

The Gospel Of Christ

AoC Network

Daily Dose Of Wisdom

AwakenWithJP/JP Sears

Victor Davis Hanson

Thomas E. Woods

The Highwire/Del Bigtree

Off The Kirb Ministries/Joe Kirby

Whaddo You Meme??

John Birch Society

Young America's Foundation

Judicial Watch/Tom Fitton

American Firebrand/Thomas Klingenstein

SexChangeRegret.com/Walt Heyer

Libs Of TikTok/Chaya Raichik

Academy Of Ideas

The Babylon Bee

VIDEOS

Event 201 Pandemic Exercise Oct. 18, 2019 Full Video

1 Hour Of The Global Elite Telling Us About
Their Future Agenda For This World

Mass Psychosis: How An Entire Population Becomes Mentally Ill

Is Government The New God? – The Religion Of Totalitarianism

Is The Mainstream Media A Threat To Freedom And Sanity?

The Big Lie – How To Enslave The World

Why Are Most People Cowards?/Obedience And
The Rise Of Authoritarianism

Candace Owens Humiliates Dr. Fauci With An Explosive Speech

Is America Turning Into A Communist Country?

Ron Johnson Rips Fauci On Senate Floor

RFK Jr. Discusses The Real Anthony Fauci/Del Bigtree

We're Approaching A Million Vaccine Injuries In The U.S./
Del Bigtree

This Is Super Disturbing! Are You Awake Now?

There Was An Unexpected 40% Increase In
'All Cause Deaths' In 2021/KUSI News
A Spike In Mysterious Deaths – Why Are Young People Suddenly
Dropping Dead Worldwide?
Florida Surgeon General Calls For Halt To Covid-19 Vaccine,
Citing Possible Cancer Risks
CDC Lies Exposed On School Masking/Saagar Enjeti
Fauci's Insane Plan To Keep Pandemic Forever/Saagar Enjeti
The Covid Cult/Thomas E. Woods
The Fact-Free Lockdown Hysteria/Thomas E. Woods
Doctors From Around The World Warn: Don't Take
Covid Vaccine
Heated Vaccine Debate – Kennedy Jr. vs Dershowitz
This Video Will Wake Up Even The Dumbest Of Sheeple
Why Socialism Never Works: A Video Marathon/PragerU
Why You Can't Trust The Mainstream Media: A Video
Marathon/PragerU
Is America Racist?: A Video Marathon, Part 1 & 2/PragerU
Race, Gender, And Culture: A Video Marathon/PragerU
Free Speech: A Video Marathon/PragerU
Fact-Check: A Video Marathon/PragerU
Every American Needs To Hear This Speech/PragerU
Restoring The Idea Of Liberty In America/Victor Davis Hanson
The Creature From Jekyll Island/G. Edward Griffin
Debunking 9/11 Debunking/David Ray Griffin
Ex-Abortion Doctor Tells The Shocking Truth About Abortion
The Kent Hovind Creation Seminar, Parts 1-7

The Creation Model vs Evolution Model, Parts 1-7/Don Patton

The Secret Code Of Creation/Jason Lisle

Science Confirms Biblical Creation/Jason Lisle

Logic And The Christian Worldview/Jason Lisle

Secrets Of The Cosmos That Confirm The Bible/Jason Lisle

Why Genesis Matters/Jason Lisle

Dinosaurs And The Bible/Jason Lisle

The Ultimate Proof Of Creation/Jason Lisle

How We Got The Bible/Jason Lisle

Atheists Will Hate This Video/Ken Ham

Science Confirms The Bible/Ken Ham

One Blood, One Race With Ken Ham

Tower Of Babel: Origin Of Races With Ken Ham

Rock Strata, Fossils And The Flood With Dr. Andrew Snelling

Wonder Of DNA By Dr. Georgia Purdom/Answers In Genesis

Noah's Ark And The Flood: Science Confirms The Bible

Dinosaurs, Dragons And The Bible/Answers In Genesis

Remarkable Evidence Of Christ's Resurrection/
Answers In Genesis

Answering Skeptics' Toughest Questions About
Christianity/Answers In Genesis

Millions Of Years: The Idea's Unscientific Origin/
NW Creation Network

Distant Starlight And Biblical Creation/Spike Psarris

The Most Convincing Evidence For A Young Earth

This Video Dismantles The Big Bang Theory

I Don't Have Enough Faith To Be An Atheist/Frank Turek

Critical Race Theory vs Christianity/Frank Turek

God And Politics/Frank Turek

What Is God Like? Look To The Heavens/Frank Turek

If God, Why Evil?/Frank Turek

Why The Bible Is Reliable/Frank Turek

We Have Been Lied To About The Origin Of Life (Renowned
Organic Chemist Speaks Out)/Daily Dose Of Wisdom

Famous Detective Investigates The Case
For Jesus/Daily Dose Of Wisdom

Origin Of Life Challenge Results + Huge
Announcement w/Lee Cronin/Dr. James Tour

We Challenge All Evolutionists To Watch This Video/
Calvin Smith

Christians, Don't Say We Didn't Warn You/Calvin Smith

Evolutionists Want You To Forget Their Dark History/
Calvin Smith

Evolutionists, You've Been Caught Lying About Fossils/
Calvin Smith

Clear Evidence Bible Prophecy Is Unfolding/AoC Network

Evidence Jesus Is The Messiah (Jonah Prophecy Revealed)/
AoC Network

There Is No Pandemic/John MacArthur

John MacArthur Lists The Effects Of Covid And Lockdowns

2022: The Covid Crisis, Totalitarianism, Antichrist/
John MacArthur

John MacArthur Says What No One
Else Will Say About The Virus

John MacArthur Says Pandemic, Masks, A Deception
to Produce State Slavery

Facts About Slavery They Don't Teach You At School/
Thomas Sowell

The Origins Of Woke/Thomas Sowell

How Schools Are Dumbing Down Young Students/
Thomas Sowell

Who Is Killing America?/Dinesh D'Souza

Academia, Hollywood, & The Media/Dinesh D'Souza

The Truths That The Left Doesn't Want You To Know/
Dinesh D'Souza

What Are The Fundamental Features Of
The Police State?/Dinesh D'Souza

The Banality Of Evil/Dinesh D'Souza

Can You Handle The Truth?/Ben Shapiro

Leftism Is Not Compassionate/Michael Knowles

Dr. Fauci: High Priest Of Progressivism/Michael Knowles

War On Reality: The Left's Plan To Redefine Life,
Marriage And Gender/Matt Walsh

The War On Masculinity/Matt Walsh

Delusions Of Gender/Matt Walsh

I Cannot Trust The Experts Because They've All Gone Insane/
Matt Walsh

A Nation Of Paranoid Lunatics Afraid Of Fresh Air/Matt Walsh

The Mask Cult Grows Even More Barbaric And Cowardly/
Matt Walsh

No I Will Not Put A Mask On My Child/Matt Walsh

Matt Walsh Confronts School Board Over Mask Mandate

Why My Kids Aren't Getting The Covid Vaccine/Matt Walsh

A Generation Descends Into Mass Psychosis/Matt Walsh

Chicago Public Schools Cordially Invite Boys Into
Girls Bathrooms/Matt Walsh

My Heroic Battle With Omicron/Matt Walsh

Mass Formation Psychosis Is Real And We're All
Living Through It/Matt Walsh

What I Learned In A Third World Country/Matt Walsh

Watch: Parent Dismantles CRT In One Fell Swoop/Matt Walsh

Male Athlete Heroically Dominates Female
Swimming Championship/Matt Walsh

Groomers Push 'Queer Inclusivity' On Preschoolers/Matt Walsh

Matt Walsh Debunks John Oliver's Home
Schooling Segment/Matt Walsh

The Victim Hierarchy By Matt Walsh

Matt Walsh Reacts To Media Matters' Hit Piece On Him

Can We Keep Silent In A World Gone Mad?/Andrew Klavan

Families Are Ditching Public School/Brett Cooper

Science, The Transgender Phenomenon, And The Young/
Abigail Shrier

I Became Transgender. Here's Why I Regret It/Walt Heyer

Jennifer Bilek/Who Is Behind The Trans Agenda?

Dr. Miriam Grossman Destroys Gender Ideology In 5 Minutes

Former Gay Reveals Truth Of LGBTQ Agenda
Flooding The Culture

The Sins Of Pride Month/Martyn Iles

How Jesus Redeemed My Gender Confusion/Dr. Linda Seiler

Lesbian Women's Studies Professor Comes To Christ: Rosaria Butterfield/The Becket Cook Show

When 'Conspiracy Theories' Turn Out To Be True/ Allie Beth Stuckey

Covid Confirmed It: Society Hates Kids/Allie Beth Stuckey

Canada's Freedom Convoy, Media Myths & The End Of Covid?/Allie Beth Stuckey

It's Vital That Christians Understand This About Critical Theory/Allie Beth Stuckey

Conversion Therapy & Canada's Assault On Christianity/Allie Beth Stuckey

How The West Was Lost... And How To Win It Back/ Allie Beth Stuckey

Exposing The Shocking Corruption Of The United Nations/Allie Beth Stuckey

Why It's A Bad Idea To Try To Disprove Christianity/ Mike Winger

Top Atheists' Best Arguments Against God. How Bad Are They?/Mike Winger

Are You A Pop-Christian Or A Real Christian?/Mike Winger

How To Get Saved/Mike Winger

How New Age & Word Of Faith Misunderstand The Bible/ Mike Winger

Slavery And The Bible!? Explained!/Mike Winger

False Teachers Exposed: Word Of Faith/Prosperity Gospel/ Justin Peters

History Of The Pentecostal/Charismatic Movement/Justin Peters

Clouds Without Water – Sessions 1, 2 & 3/Justin Peters

Is Joel Osteen Merely Not Recommended, Or Is He
A False Teacher?/Justin Peters

Mysticism: The Deadly Dangers Of Trusting Personal Experience
Over Biblical Authority/Justin Peters

The Essential Church: An Interview With John MacArthur/
Justin Peters

Romans 13 And James Coates/Justin Peters

The Gospel/Justin Peters

Interview With Former Roman Catholic Mike Gendron/
Justin Peters

Warning! Catholics Must Leave Their Religion/Mike Gendron

Roman Catholicism's Drift Into Apostasy/Mike Gendron

Effective Witnessing To Roman Catholics/Mike Gendron

Marx vs Spurgeon/Larry Alex Taunton

Understanding The Woke Mind/Larry Alex Taunton

What Really Happened At The White House
This Week?/Larry Alex Taunton

Full Speech: Tucker Carlson's Last Address Before Leaving Fox

They Hate The Truth/Tucker Carlson

Here's What You Need To Remember When
Debating The Left/Tucker Carlson

Laugh In The Face Of Authoritarianism/Tucker Carlson

Bret Weinstein Exposes The World Health Organization's
Dark Agenda/Tucker Carlson

Here's What Really Happened On January 6th/Tucker Carlson

Tucker Carlson And Douglas Murray (Full Interview)

Tucker Carlson Tonight Ep. 43 11/30/23

Vince Everett Ellison: Will Blacks Go To Hell For The
Democrat Party? Part 1 & 2/The Carl Jackson Show

Vince Everett Ellison Live At The June High School Conference

Allen West At Alabama: How The Left Destroyed Black America

Harvard, Hamas, And The Barbaric Death
Of Discourse In The West

Relativism: The Worst Belief Ever With Greg Koukl/
Alisa Childers

Mere Christianity (Audiobook)/C. S. Lewis

The Pilgrim's Progress (Audiobook)/John Bunyan

The Law (Audiobook)/Frederic Bastiat

Biden's 17 Greatest Achievements So Far!/JP Sears

Is Klaus Schwaub The Most Dangerous Man In The World?/
JP Sears

Defending The American Way Of Life – The War – Part 1/
Thomas Klingenstein

The Big Lie: America Is Racist – The War – Part 2/
Thomas Klingenstein

War Is A Time For Fighting – The War – Part 3/
Thomas Klingenstein

A Self-Loathing Country Cannot Survive – The War – Part 4/
Thomas Klingenstein

Nazis, Fascists And Democrats/Bill Whittle

A Christian Response To Wokeness (Full Video)/Noelle Mering

Michael Shellenberger's Guide To Escaping The Woke Matrix

It's Time: Calls Grow To Ditch 'Diversity, Equity And Inclusion'
Constitution 101/Hillsdale College
The Secret Religion That Rules The World (5 Hrs. 17 min.)/
Altian Childs

SERMONS

Humanity On Trial/John MacArthur
The Gospel Satisfies The Sinner's Need/John MacArthur
The Truth About Hell/John MacArthur
Saved Or Self-Deceived, Part 1 & 2/John MacArthur
Abortion And The Campaign For Immorality/John MacArthur
Homosexuality And The Campaign For Immorality/
John MacArthur
When God Abandons A Nation/John MacArthur
The Disastrous Sin Of Lying/John MacArthur
Why The World Rejects God's Word/John MacArthur
Why You Can Trust Scripture/John MacArthur
The Pope And The Papacy/John MacArthur
Roman Catholic False Gospel/John MacArthur
Exposing The Idolatry Of Mary Worship/John MacArthur
Explaining The Heresy Of The Catholic Mass, Part 1 & 2/
John MacArthur
Religion And Its Victims/John MacArthur
Becoming A Better You?/John MacArthur
Does The Bible Permit A Woman To Preach?/John MacArthur
Social Justice And The Gospel, Parts 1 – 4/John MacArthur

Christian Deconstruction, Part 1 & 2/John MacArthur

Testing The Spirits/John MacArthur

Who's To Blame For The Riots?/John MacArthur

Why Did Jesus Have To Die?/John MacArthur

Divine Barriers To Superficial Seekers/John MacArthur

Who's Ashamed Of Whom?/John MacArthur

We Must Obey God Rather Than Men/John MacArthur

When Government Rewards Evil And Punishes Good/
John MacArthur

The Truth Shall Set You Free/John MacArthur

The Truth Of God's Word/Ken Ham

Is Gay The New Black?/Voddie Baucham

Fault Lines: Critical Race Theory/Voddie Baucham

Biblical Justice vs Social Justice/Voddie Baucham

Why You Can Believe The Bible/Voddie Baucham

The Necessity Of Absolute Truth/Voddie Baucham

Defending The Faith In A Hostile World/Voddie Baucham

Man And Woman By God's Design/Voddie Baucham

Why The Good News Is So Good/Voddie Baucham

The Modern Church's Sissified Jesus/Voddie Baucham

Dragons Abounding: The Great Errors Confronting
The Church/Voddie Baucham

Why I Believe In The Resurrection/Voddie Baucham

What Is Truth? The Remedy For A Culture in Chaos/
Mike Riccardi

The Truth Shall Set You Free/Albert Mohler

Learn The Bible In 24 Hours, Parts 1 – 24/Chuck Missler

The Cycle Of Nations/Chuck Missler

Hidden Treasures Of The Bible/Chuck Missler

Armor For The Age Of Deceit, Part 1 & 2/Chuck Missler

The True Gospel vs Prosperity Theology/Costi Hinn

The Protestant Reformation vs The New Apostolic
Reformation/Costi Hinn

Refuting Catholic Authority/Mike Winger

Unbiblical Stuff The Catholic Church Teaches/Mike Winger

Homosexuality, Parts 1 – 4/Mike Winger

A Biblical Response To The 'Transing' Of America/
Gary Hamrick

Israel, Hamas, And End Times/Ezekiel 38/Gary Hamrick

The Tyranny Of Totalitarianism – Romans 13:1 – 4/
James Coates

Letter To The American Church – Eric Metaxas/Calvary Church

This Is How Our Society Is Actively Rejecting God/Martyn Iles

The Shocking Truth About Babylon/Martyn Iles

Self Delusion – Charles Spurgeon Sermon

The Story Of Reality/Greg Koukl

BIBLIOGRAPHY

1. www.goodreads.com/quotes/584507.
2. www.goodreads.com/quotes/10579799.
3. www.goodreads.com/quotes/39025.
4. www.goodreads.com/quotes/52626.
5. www.goodreads.com/quotes/33679.
6. www.goodreads.com/quotes/7471034.
7. Holy Bible: New American Standard Bible. 1995. La Habra, CA. The Lockman Foundation.
8. Bergman, Jerry. "One of the Most Widely Used Quotes by D.M.S. Watson Vindicated. www.assets.answersingenesis.org/doc/articles/arj/v14/quote_watson.pdf. Answers Research Journal 14 (2021)
9. www.quotes.net/quote/12135.
10. www.azquotes.com/author/7835-Arthur_Keith.
11. www.creationism.org/english/quotes_en.htm.
12. www.creationtoday.org/scientists-quotes-about-evolution.
13. www.goodreads.com/quotes/7838107-the-extreme-rarity-of-transitional-forms-in-the-fossil-record.
14. www.answersingenesis.org/theory-of-evolution/a-designer-is-unscientific/.
15. www.godordirt.com/home-school-zone/fossils-refute-evolution-2/.
16. www.creation.com/michael-ruse-evolution-is-a-religion.
17. www.creation.com/origin-of-life-a-matter-of-faith.
18. www.creation.com/amazing-admission-lewontin-quote.
19. www.azquotes.com/author/29962-Louis_T_Moore.
20. www.nwcreation.net/evolutionquotes.html.

21. www.nwcreation.net/evolutionquotes.html.

22. Darwin, Charles. On The Origin of Species. A Penn State Electronic Classics Series Publication. Page 173. www.f.waseda.jp/sidoli/Darwin_Origin_Of_Species.pdf.

23. Darwin, Charles. On The Origin of Species. A Penn State Electonic Series Publication. Page 158. www.f.waseda.jp/sidoli/Darwin_Origin_of_Species.pdf.

24. www.creationliberty.com/articles/evolution5th.php.

25. www.answersingenesis.org/scopes-trial/inherit-the-wind-an-historical-analysis.

26. De Camp, L. Sprague. The Great Monkey Trial. Doubleday, 1968.27.

27. "cognitive dissonance." www.merriam-webster.com/dictionary/cognitive%20dissonance. Merriam-Webster.com 2021

28. "cognitive dissonance." www.britannica.com/cognitive-dissonance. Britannica.com 2021

29. Andersen, Hans Christian. The Emperor's New Clothes. Denmark, 1837. www.genius.com/Hc-andersen-the-emperors-new-clothes-annotated.

30. www.goodreads.com/7246592-power-tends-to-corrupt-and-absolute-power-corrupts-absolutely-great.

31. Rockefeller, David. www.goodreads.com/work/quotes/17899-memoirs. Memoirs. Random House, 2002. Page 405

32. www.goodreads.com/author/quotes/9951.David_Rockefeller.

33. Ballasy, Nicholas. "The 'affirmative task' before us is to 'create a new world order.'" YouTube, uploaded by Nicholas Ballasy, 5 Apr. 2013. www.youtube.com/watch?v=b1AMYHHAXhl.

34. Talbott, Strobe. "America Abroad: The Birth of The Global Nation." Time, 20 July. 1992. www.content.time.com/time/subscriber/article/0,33009,976015,00.html

35. "Henry Kissinger Calls for Barack Obama To Create A New World Order." BitChute, uploaded by Not-2-B-4-Got-10, 22 Dec. 2020, www.bitchute.com/video/OLsSkWiAhlkp/

36. Jasper, William F. "Global Gorby." The New American, 30 Oct. 1995. www.thenewamerican.com/global-gorby/

37. Schaub, Eric. "Infamous Quote by Peter Hoagland." LibertyTree,

www.libertytree.ca/quotes/Peter.Hoagland.Quote.0FD8

38. Jasper, William F. "The War on Sovereignty." The New American, 17 May 2004. www.thenewamerican.com/the-war-on-sovereignty

39. www.azquotes.com/author/37751-Brock_Chisholm

40. "Top 25 Quotes by David Spangler." www.azquotes.com/author/22648-David_Spangler

41. Schaub, Eric. "Infamous Quote by James Paul Warburg." LibertyTree, www.libertytree.ca/quotes/James.Warburg.Quote.BC08

42. "Tony Blair Speech on Faith And Globalisation." Sewa UK, www.sewauk.org/tony-blair-speech-on-faith-and-globalisation

43. www.goodreads.com/quotes/162691-the-technotronic-era-involves-the-gradual-appearance-of-a-more

44. Davido. "What Will Government Do with Bitcoin?" Coinmonks, www.medium.com/coinmonks/what-will-happen-with-bitcoin-5b284b44b19

45. "Address Before the 45th Session of the United Nations General Assembly in New York, New York." www.presidency.ucsb.edu/documents/address-before-the-united-nations-general-assembly-new-york-new-york

46. Schaub, Eric. "Infamous Quote by Mayer Amschel Rothschild." LibertyTree, www.libertytree.ca/quotes/Mayer.Amschel.Rothschild.Quote.8BED

47. Our Republic, www.ourrepubliconline.com/author/49

48. "Al Gore talks climate crisis: 'This is the time for a great reset.'" Yahoo News, 19 June 2020. www.news.yahoo.com/al-gore-talks-climate-crisis-132403941.html

49. "WEF BILLS DAVOS 2021 AS THE 'GREAT RESET.'" by AFP. Breitbart, 3 June 2020. www.breitbart.com/news/wef-bills-davos-2021-as-the-great-reset/ "Now Comes the Davos Global Economy 'Great Reset.' What Happens After the Covid-19 Plandemic?" by Engdahl, F. William. 18 July 2020. www.themadtruther.com/2020/07/18/now-comes-the-davos-global-economy-great-reset-what-happens-after-the-covid-19-plandemic/

50. Haskins, Justin. "Al Gore, John Kerry, Other World Leaders Call for Radical 'Great Reset' of Capitalism." The Epoch Times, 6 July 2020.

www.theepochtimes.com/al-gore-john-kerry-other-world-leaders-call-for-radical-great-reset-of-capitalism_3412203.html

51. "A Great Reset: The Economic Forum Suggests a Different Post-Covid Future for The World." European Business Magazine, 17 Sep. 2020. www.europeanbusinessmagazine.com/technology/great-reset-world-economic-forum-suggests-different-post-covid-future-world/, www.weforum.org/focus/the-great-reset, World Economic Forum

52. Inman, Phillip. "Pandemic is chance to reset global economy, says Prince Charles." The Guardian, 3 June 2020. www.theguardian.com/uk-news/2020/jun/03/pandemic-is-chance-to-reset-global-economy-says-prince-charles

53. World Economic Forum. "Great Reset/Kristalina Georgieva/How will history judge this moment?" YouTube, uploaded by World Economic Forum Video, 3 June 2020. www.youtube.com/watch?v=FX3lwg-DZ-z8

54. World Economic Forum. "The Great Reset." YouTube, uploaded by World Economic Forum, 3 June 2020. www.youtube.com/watch?v=8rAiTDQ-NVY

55. "The Great Reset. You'll Own Nothing and Be Happy. World Economic Forum Commercial. Davos Group." YouTube, uploaded by Son of a Bear: Foraging and Bushcraft, 31 Jan. 2021. www.youtube.com/watch?v=aztvWxRKqDQ

56. "The Speech that Killed John F. Kennedy – JFK." Bing, uploaded by GloomyHouse, originally uploaded on YouTube, 26 Mar. 2018. www.bing.com/videos/search?q=the+speech+that+got+kennedy+killed &docid=6079937581366679460&mid=EA86A1FCC973FB469242EA86 A1...

57. Schaub, Eric. www.libertytree.ca/quotes/Larry.P.McDonald. Quote.5040, "Quote by Larry P. McDonald." LibertyTree

58. Baldwin, Chuck. "The Grinch Who Stole Conservatism." Conservative Truth, 16 Aug. 2010. www.conservativetruth.org/article.php?id=1974

59. Zember, Mordechai. "Council On Foreign Relations Is an Elite Cabal." NewsWithViews.com, 22 Jan. 2006. www.citizensoftheamericanconstitution.net/Tyranny%20Files/Addition al%20Resources/

Additional%20Resources/Recommended%20Readin g/CF...

60. Newman, Alex. "Deep State Behind the Deep State: CFR, Trilaterals, Bilderberg." The New American, 30 Oct. 2017. www.thenewamerican.com/deep-state-behind-the-deep-state-cfr-trilaterals-bilderberg/

61. www.goodreads.com/quotes/8716334-the-real-menace-of-our-republic-is-the-invisible-government

62. "Ancient Banking Secret Revealed – How Banks Manufacture Money Out of Nothing." www.ancientbankingsecret.com/blog/

63. www.goodreads.com/quotes/161878-history-records-that-the-money-changers-have-used-every-form

64. www.goodreads.com/quotes/162689-the-real-truth-of-the-matter-is-as-you-and

65. www.citatis.com/a35140/17530f/

66. www.azquotes.com/quote/101819

67. www.goodreads.com/quotes/199916-some-of-the-biggest-men-in-the-united-states-in,
www.themoneymasters.com/the-money-masters/famous-quotations-on-banking/

68. www.goodreads.com/quotes/34770-it-is-well-enough-that-people-of-the-nation-do

69. The Ethical Economy, www.theethicaleconomy.com/louis-t-mcfadden

70. www.goodreads.com/quotes/288058-whoever-controls-the-volume-of-money-in-our-country-is

71. Op Ed News, www.opednews.com/Quotations/The-money-powers-prey-upon-the-by-Lincoln-Abraham-111016-448.html

72. www.azquotes.com/quote/679657

73. "Before a Joint Session of Congress – 11 September 1990 [Historical Speeches TV]", YouTube, uploaded by Historical Speeches TV, 6 Dec. 2018. (quote in question comes at the 15 minute, 40 second mark) www.youtube.com/watch?v=meXladt85oA

74. "George Bush Sr. New World Order Live Speech Sept 11, 1991" YouTube, uploaded by MrWolfenz, 4 Dec. 2011. www.youtube.com/watch?v=byxeOG_pZ1o

75. www.azquotes.com/author/3422-Walter_Cronkite

76. "The American people don't believe anything until they see it on

television." www.barrypopik.com/index.php/new_york_city/entry/
the_american_people_dont_believe/ The Big Apple, 30 Oct. 2019.

77. "Scenarios for the Future of Technology and International Development." pages 16, 18, 19, 21. www.truthcomestolight.com/
wp-content/uploads/2020/07/Rockefeller-Foundation-2010-Scenari-
os-for-the-Future-of-Technology-and-Intern...

78. Osip, Mike. "Dr Fauci – There will be a surprise outbreak WHOA!
Dr. Fauci in 2017". YouTube, 4 Apr 2020. uploaded by Mike Osip.
www.youtube.com/watch?v=zu2Ftcv6u3w

79. "March 2020: Dr. Anthony Fauci talks with Jon LaPook about Covid-
19." YouTube, 8 Mar. 2020. uploaded by 60 Minutes. www.youtube.
com/watch?v=PRa6t_e7dgl

80. Baker, Peter. The New York Times, 17 Mar. 2020. "U.S. Virus Plan
Anticipates 18-Month Pandemic and Widespread Shortages." www.
nytimes.com/2020/03/17/us/politics/trump-coronavirus-plan.html

81. Haber, Sagi. " NOBEL prize winner Dr. Kary Mullis says: Dr. Fauci is
LIAR a con man." YouTube, 11 Dec. 2020. uploaded by Sagi Haber.
www.youtube.com/watch?v=W8FYWzkR1ek

82. Miltimore, Jon. "3 Studies That Show Lockdowns Are Ineffective at
Slowing Covid-19." Fee Stories, 9 Dec. 2020. www.fee.org/articles/3-
studies-that-show-lockdowns-are-ineffective-at-slowing-covid-19/

83. Tucker, Jeffrey A. "Even a Military-Enforced Quarantine Can't Stop
the Virus, Study Reveals." American Institute for Economic Research,
13 Nov. 2020. www.aier.org/article/even-a-military-enforced-quaran-
tine-cant-stop-the-virus-study-reveals/

84. Fox, Megan. "Bombshell E-mails Reveal That Fauci Wasn't Being
Straight with the American People." PJ Media, 2 June 2021. www.
pjmedia.com/columns/megan-fox/2021/06/02/emails-reveal-that-fau-
ci-wasnt-being-straight-with-the-american-people-n1451475

85. Reynolds, Stewart. "Reasons To Not Wear A Face Mask." You-
Tube, uploaded by brittlestar. 10 July 2020. www.youtube.com/
watch?v=TIXoAuU9xAe

86. Vistaprint. "This is not a mask – Vistaprint." YouTube, uploaded by
Vistaprint. 22 June 2020. www.youtube.com/watch?v=DoJ4OGiA1qs

87. Schwab, Tim. "Journalism's Gates Keepers." Columbia Journalism

Review, 21 Aug. 2020. www.cjr.org/criticism/gates-foundation-jour-nalism-funding.php

88.   "'The CDC is actually a vaccine company' – Robert F. Kennedy Jr.", YouTube, uploaded by RT America. 31 Jan. 2020. www.youtube.com/watch?v=5CfLDXpC324

89.   "'...normalcy only returns when we've largely vaccinated the entire global population' – Bill Gates.", YouTube, uploaded by Gene Lara-tonda. 18 Apr. 2020. www.youtube.com/watch?v=ND6KcuLJv5k

90.   Vigilant Citizen. "Bill Gates Calls for a 'Digital Certificate' to Iden-tify Who Received Covid-19 Vaccine." www.lewrockwell.com/2020/no_author/bill-gates-calls-for-a-digital-certificate-to-identify-who-re-ceived-covid-19-vaccine/, LewRockwel.com, 3 Apr. 2020.

91.   "Bill Gates: We are injecting GMO into little kids' arms." YouTube, uploaded by Truth Monitor. 13 May 2020. www.youtube.com/watch?v=EvoBwgd1988

92.   "Bill Gates: Population Reduction @ Ted 2010." YouTube, uploaded by SupergirlFan. 27 May 2010. (at the 2 minute mark) www.youtube.com/watch?v=LmzeYYWntxw

93.   Belvedere, Matthew J. "Bill Gates: My 'best investment' turned $10 billion into $200 billion worth of economic benefit." CNBC, 23 Jan. 2019. www.cnbc.com/2019/01/23/bill-gates-turns-10-billion-into-200-billion-worth-of-economic-benefit.html

94.   "Robert F. Kennedy Jr. on the Bill Gates Vaccination Agenda." Scien-tists For Wired Technology. www.scientists4wiredtech.com/2020/04/robert-f-kennedy-jr-on-the-bill-gates-vaccination-agenda/

95.   Chappell, Bill. "Instagram Bars Robert F. Kennedy Jr. For Spread-ing Vaccine Misinformation." KPBS, 11 Feb. 2021. www.kpbs.org/news/2021/feb/11/instagram-bars-robert-f-kennedy-jr-for-spreading/

96.   "Remarks to the Congressional Black Caucus Prayer Breakfast." The American Presidency Project. 11 Sep. 2004. www.presidency.ucsb.edu/documents/remarks-the-congressional-black-caucus-prayer-breakfast

97.   "Anton LaVey's Deathbed Confession." YouTube, uploaded by Ste-phen King. 11 July 2009. www.youtube.com/watch?v=5sZcUsrbvfl

98.   Shaw, Solomon B. Dying Testimonies of the Saved and Unsaved, Reformation Publishing, 2000, originally published in 1898.

99. www.quotesgram.com/john-huss-quotes/

100. Walsh, Matt. "My Heroic Battle with Omicron." YouTube, uploaded by Matt Walsh. 3 Jan. 2022. (6 minute 45 second mark) www.youtube.com/watch?v=JMusLfvla7M

www.ingramcontent.com/pod-product-compliance
Lightning Source LLC
Chambersburg PA
CBHW071713120626
46550CB00001B/214